Your RETIREMENT, *your* WAY

Why it takes more than money to live your dream

Alan Bernstein, L.C.S.W., and John Trauth, M.B.A.

New York   Chicago   San Francisco   Lisbon   London   Madrid   Mexico City
Milan   New Delhi   San Juan   Seoul   Singapore   Sydney   Toronto

Library of Congress Cataloging-in-Publication Data

Bernstein, Alan, 1941-
    Your retirement, your way : why it takes more than money to live your dream /
by Alan Bernstein and John Trauth.
       p. cm.
    Includes bibliographical references.
    ISBN 0-07-146787-4 (alk. paper)
    1. Retirement—Planning. 2. Retirement income--Planning. 3. Finance, Personal.
    I. Trauth, John. II. Title.

HQ1062.B434 2007
646.7'9—dc22   2006024763

*To Dr. Louis Ormont, whose patient guidance through the years encouraged
me to develop and thrive. And to Richard Nelson Bolles who directed my
attention to key areas in mind and spirit. My deepest gratitude to you both.*

—ALAN BERNSTEIN

To Astrid, Elizabeth, Lisa, John, Libby, Eric, Carrie, and Keoki.

—JOHN TRAUTH

1 2 3 4 5 6 7 8 9 10 11 12 13 14 15   DOC/DOC   0 9 8 7 6

ISBN 13: 978-0-07-146787-2
ISBN 10:   0-07-146787-4

Interior design by Scott Rattray
Interior illustrations by Gail Rattray

McGraw-Hill books are available at special quantity discounts to use as premiums and
sales promotions, or for use in corporate training programs. For more information, please
write to the Director of Special Sales, Professional Publishing, McGraw-Hill, Two Penn
Plaza, New York, NY 10121-2298. Or contact your local bookstore.

This book is printed on acid-free paper.

Contents

Preface

Alan Bernstein

I am always intrigued when I notice myself avoiding unpleasant ideas. And retirement was one of them.

Although I had taken some initial steps to reduce my private office hours, I was at the same time expanding my corporate consulting practice. None of this was done with deliberation—it was just sort of happening. As I mused about this, I reminded myself that one of my friends, John Trauth, had taken early retirement and then spent the better part of the next year in France. He and his wife, Astrid, had shared a lifelong dream of becoming fluent in French, and they did it! When we talked about his trip, one of the striking things to me was his deliberateness—he had wanted to do this, he planned it (including subleasing his properties), and it fit comfortably within an overall life strategy.

I was stirred by the difference in our thought processes. While I was drawn to where and how I (and others) get stuck, John was drawn to strategies for moving ahead. I observed that most of my friends and I were, in essence, denying that anything had to be planned for our future. We were (on the whole) healthy and professionally successful and would (we apparently assumed) stay that way forever. We would occasionally have brief conversations about "not being able to afford to retire" but the conversations would quickly move on to other topics.

I thought about John's and my Birkman® profiles (you will be introduced to The Birkman Method® in Chapter 4), and how my Blue, thoughtful and contemplative, interests intersected with John's Red, goal-directed, behavior. This could mean, I speculated, a spectrum of approaches for this new phase of life called retirement.

I had reviewed the retirement books available at my local bookstore and eyeballed what seemed to be an endless array of financial self-help books. It seemed that the underlying supposition about retirement was that happiness was generated by financial preparation; if you had a sufficient revenue stream, you would just retire and love it. However, I knew from my psychotherapy practice that the presenting problem ("I don't have enough money to retire") is frequently far removed from the real, underlying problem. In our society, it seems, anxieties about money are more acceptable than anxieties about loss of purpose and identity or about assuming new social roles. The few books I found with some insight into the more subtle issues of retirement preparation either presented anecdotal information ("here is what Mr. or Ms. X did") or general psychological principles without prescriptive applications.

When I consulted the research literature, I found some shocking statistics. Retirees have the highest divorce rate in the United States! Also, 40 percent of people surveyed five years after retirement reported feelings of "sadness," "worry," and "boredom" and acknowledged that they were happier before retiring. Only 19 percent felt "adventurous" or "empowered."

The "strugglers," who were the largest class of retirees, wished they had spent more time in "planning and preparation."* I speculated whether a book along the lines of *Guide to Your Career*, an earlier guide I had written for college graduates looking for their first jobs, might be useful, both for me and for other potential retirees.

As I talked with John, now my coauthor, and the people at McGraw-Hill, I began to see this book as a potential new approach to retirement decision making. Our approach would use the tools of psychotherapy that I apply in my work (Have I been here before? What is stopping me from moving forward? What are my resources for this transition?) combined with the tools of goal-directed strategic planning with which John is familiar. John and I speculated that our collective resources might create a powerful new approach to retirement planning, combining proven self-analysis techniques to determine needs and desires in retirement with an individually designed strategic-planning process to create a customized retirement lifestyle to fulfill those very same needs and desires.

At the same time, this approach might prove helpful in the battle between endless contemplation and inaction versus acting only to counteract a feeling of passivity and thereby proceeding without all necessary information.

We were excited by the combination of our strengths and decided to test an initial program at John's alma mater, the Amos Tuck Graduate School of Business at Dartmouth College. To our surprise, about 30 percent of our audience was under age forty-five! We found ourselves buoyed by the expe-

---

*From "The New Retirement Mindscape" study by Ameriprise Financial (formerly American Express Financial Advisors).

rience of leading this seminar while sharing our own experiences. We decided to pursue and refine our approach. Out of this process, we birthed this book, which we hope will help you recognize and draw on resources that you may never have recognized. In addition, we give you a system for transforming those resources into the pillars of your future retirement—to create a truly fulfilling life, custom-designed for you and you alone.

John and I look forward to this exciting exploration with you!

John and I wrote our chapters separately, but, of course, in consultation. You will find the name of the chapter's author below the title of each chapter. All characters in illustrative stories are based on our practices and are real individuals with their names changed.

Alan's Acknowledgments

- First and foremost, to my First Reader, who has mastered the art of constructive criticism, my dear wife, Anne, and to her parents, Peter and Nanschi Lesch, and their progeny, Rose and Lynn, and Derek and Lisa. Always a joy to spend time with you.
- To my daughter Rachel and her wonderful husband, Brad, and their delightful children, Grace, Kiley, Maisie, and Luke, perhaps best known as my grandchildren.
- To my brother Carl, a tireless supporter of me and the University of Michigan (I hope in that order) and Harriette, and their wonderful daughter, my niece, Elizabeth.
- To the Birkman organization, which has supported my work from the beginning—a heartfelt thanks to Roger for creating the Method® and Sharon for carrying on the tradition in so generous a manner.
- To the University of Michigan, which educated me and, come to think of it, almost all my nearest and dearest, and especially to Dean Evan Caminker, Laurie

Boddie, Kathy Noble, Kathleen Stevens, and Barbara Mulay, all of whom patiently listened to me explain the importance of my retirement philosophy and, unbelievably, fed back helpful and creative ideas.

- My professional colleagues and friends, Larry Epstein, Jim Behrman, Bonnie Jacobson, Emily Nash, Gita Vaid, Richard Friedman, and Joseph Merlino who remind me through their patience and empathy that we are in the business of handling souls.

- To George Gewirtz, who, as I regularly tell him, reminds me that we will always be fifteen years olds taking a stroll on Ocean Parkway going over life's key points. I'm lucky to have you as a friend.

- To Tom Gefell, who read the complete text and ably offered constructive criticism balanced with enthusiastic appreciation.

- To John Aherne, our tireless editor, who represented us ably at McGraw-Hill at every turn.

- To Stacey Glick, our agent—this book is largely yours.

- And to Alexia Paul, with special thanks, who read, edited, wrote, and shaped my chapters at every turn— this book wouldn't exist without you.

- My suitemates, Robyn Abramson, Donna Jacobs, and Loren Lortscher, who make opening the door to the day a looked-forward-to experience.

- Sam James, for his incisive critique that reshaped the book. Thank you.

John's Acknowledgments

Like Alan, many people also contributed to helping me write this book, and I thank you all, particularly the following individuals:

- To my good friends in the financial services industry in San Francisco, particularly Margarita Perry of Merrill Lynch and Susan Morse, Kevin Gahagan, and Norm Boone of Mosaic Financial Partners.
- To Dean Paul Danos and Andy Steele of the Amos Tuck School of Business who allowed us to pretest this concept with Tuck alumni when it was still in the idea phase.
- To Bronwyn Belling who worked on the Development Fund's pioneering work to develop and test the concept of reverse mortgages and continues that good work to this day with AARP.
- To Dean Gary Williams, dean of the University of San Francisco's Graduate School of Business, and Senior Associate Dean Eugene Muscat who believed in the

idea of this book and helped me approach the local
USF alumni groups interested in retirement planning.
- To George Schofield, president of the Clarity Group,
  who is a leading thinker in healthy and adaptive aging
  issues and who helped expand my thinking in this field.

But especially three very special people:

- To Kathy Kenny, with whom I did so much good work
  together over the years, setting up community lending
  programs, establishing new nonprofit mortgage
  banking corporations, and creating their initial
  business plans and strategic plans.
- To Jim Horan, author of *The One Page Business Plan*.
  Not only have Kathy and I used his excellent material
  extensively with our nonprofit clients, but Jim was very
  helpful in giving me his perspective on this book on
  several occasions, advice which proved to be sage
  indeed.
- Finally, and most importantly, to my wife, Astrid, who
  has always been there for me and willing to give me
  whatever support I needed, not only for this book but
  for all the other things that I decided to take on in my
  life. She always had confidence in me, and for that I
  owe her all the success I have achieved. I couldn't have
  done it without her. Our life together is wonderful, and
  our adventure continues.

Welcome to Your NewLife

John Trauth

I don't want to get to the end of my life and find I have just lived the length of it. I want to have lived the width of it as well.

—Diane Ackerman, author

There are two major transitions in life: from student to the workforce and from the workforce to retirement. We all spend enormous effort and countless years preparing to become productive members of society; however, when it comes to retirement, most people just "wing it," hoping that their dreams will magically come true. So it is not surprising that many successful people "fail" at retirement. According to a recent survey, 40 percent of recent retirees in North America said they were happier when they were working.

Don't let this happen to you. Retirement could well represent another third of your life. Do you really want to be unhappy and unfulfilled for thirty years?

In spite of what you've read in many other books and articles, retirement is not primarily about the money. While money is obviously very important, it's really all about determining *the life* that will make you feel fulfilled, vital, happy and alive, then developing a plan to get you there.

But you need more than just one plan. Because retirement is a major phase of life and life is multidimensional, you need many plans. And you need to put them all together into a Master Plan. *Webster's Third New International Dictionary of the English Language* defines a master plan as "an overall plan into which the details of other specific plans are fitted."

Think of it this way. You didn't take just one course in college or grad school to prepare for your career, you took many different courses and prepared on many different levels. You need to do the same thing now to prepare for retirement. You need to make a number of plans because you need to look at your potential retirement lifestyle from many different angles and then assemble all these plans together into a Master Plan that will guide you on your retirement journey.

Obviously, this will take some work. But *Your Retirement, Your Way* makes it fun and easy. We provide you with a structured process that will give you the power to take your future life into your own hands and create the ideal retirement lifestyle for yourself, unique to your own interests, personality, style, and situation. First, you will undertake a comprehensive personal assessment that includes The Birkman Method®, a proven system used by Fortune 500 companies. Then, with a clear understanding of your personal strengths and needs in retirement, you will proceed through an individually tailored strategic-planning process to envision your ideal "NewLife" and create your customized Master Plan to make it a reality.

Your Retirement, Your Way gives you all the tools you need to make your retirement dreams come true.

How and Why It Works

Celebrities know that they have a "persona" to manage. Their managers and agents train them to think of themselves as a personal corporation (most of them actually are) and then organize, promote, and manage that entity to maximize its potential. This book will help you to think of yourself the same way. First, you will do some guided self-analysis to learn more about your style, needs, and interests. You probably took these tests earlier in life when you were trying to decide what career would be best for you. Now it is time to do this again, because you have changed. You have matured. You have accomplished many things, and some of those things may no longer be of interest to you. You have also probably had to decide *not* to do some things that you wanted to do but didn't have time for, given the other decisions and commitments you made. When you retire, you will have additional time, and you can structure that time as you wish to pursue those interests and dreams that you have had to postpone. Thus, in the first half of this book, you will follow the advice of the Delphic oracle, which counseled, "Know thyself."

In the second half of the book, you will take this knowledge and apply it to creating the plans and activities that will guide you toward realizing your dreams. But these are not plans that will sit on a shelf. Your individually tailored NewLife Master Plan will be a living plan, something you will look at every day and periodically evaluate and update. You will create what David Corbett, president of New Directions in Boston, calls "dreams with deadlines." But this time, the deadlines will be your own. And you can periodically evaluate them and change them if you wish. Your plan will give you a system for doing just that.

While you may be ending a full-time professional career, you are also beginning a new phase of life with infinite and wonderful possibilities, beyond anything that was possible before! Your customized NewLife Master Plan will help you take full advantage of those possibilities.

Who Are We to Tell You What to Do?

Let me tell you how this book came about. In 1995, I "retired" at the ripe age of fifty-two. I had been working in the financial world in San Francisco, running a company that developed large-scale community lending programs. Basically, we created statewide bank lending consortia, through which banks, financial institutions, and others would pledge capital (and also share risk) to finance projects in disadvantaged areas. As the areas improved, this created new opportunities for the banks to lend additional capital directly. The work went very well, and we raised $650 million in pledged capital, but it was very intense and stressful. So, at the successful conclusion of creating a $50 million statewide small-business lending program in California, I retired.

Ever since college, when I first started traveling abroad, one of my goals was to become fluent in another language. In spite of many attempts, it hadn't happened. So with the enthusiastic support of my wife, who was at the time writing a book about the Avignon popes, we packed our bags and moved to France for a year. I went back to school, to the Sorbonne in Paris, and studied French language and culture. Six months later, after completing my studies, we moved to Provence to try living in the French countryside.

The time was rich, and I learned a lot during that year. I learned to speak French, eventually fluently, as well as read and write the language, and we made many lifelong friends. More importantly, I learned many things about myself. I learned that I was more a city boy than a country boy, preferring to live in or near a big city, with all of its cultural attractions, and vacation in the country, rather than the other way around. I learned that being on perpetual vacation was not all that it was cracked up to be. I learned the difficulties of living in a different culture; on the other hand, I learned that living abroad for an extended period challenges your perspective in interesting ways and makes you more inclined to question some of the basic beliefs you took for granted about your own life than would otherwise be the case. I also learned that I wanted to live on American soil and to continue to contribute and be productive.

The question for me was how to reinvent myself when we returned home.

Soon after we got back to San Francisco, my good friend and the coauthor of this book, Alan Bernstein, and I went on our annual camping trip in the California Sierra Mountains. Alan is a psychotherapist based in New York City. We met twenty-four years ago on an Outward Bound program in Minnesota that combined ten days of strenuous outdoor canoeing, portaging, and camping with professionally facilitated evening fireside discussions about midcareer renewal. It was a great experience.

Because I was born in New York and my family still lives in Manhattan, I return often, and Alan and I continued to see each other frequently and became close friends. For the last twenty-plus years, we have spent a week together each year hiking, camping, skiing, sculling, or doing other athletic activities.

Before we set out on this particular trip, Alan sent me a personality profile test, called the Birkman® (which you will encounter in Chapter 4), and told me to "take it!" When I asked why, he said, "Because you will find it helpful in figuring out what you want to do for the rest of your life." I took it and sent him the completed questionnaire. He sent it to Texas for scoring and brought the results along on our camping trip.

We were camped at a small, secluded lake in Desolation Wilderness, a remote and beautiful area at 8,000 feet in the Sierras near Lake Tahoe, when Alan pulled out the results of my test from his backpack. I sat on a rock, overlooking Middle Velma Lake and, to my astonishment, learned from my Birkman® results that the ideal job for me was exactly the job I had had before I retired, which I had created for myself! But the test also showed me some interests that I had not pursued, which were still appealing to me. And it showed me clearly what I would *not* be happy doing.

To make a long story short, I went home, hung out my shingle as an individual financial consultant, and quickly found the same kind of work that I had done before. My new work arrangements gave me just as much pleasure as before without the stress of having to manage a company and meet a monthly payroll. I did not need to work, because I was financially secure, but I wanted to. The difference was that now I only took on the work I wanted to do, and it was no problem if months went by with nothing that met my new standards. I also resolved to limit my work to half-time, which would free up the other half to pursue other interests that I previously had had to exclude. Today, I am happier than ever and even more productive in my work, with much less stress. I am also president of the board of my athletic club's foundation, which raises money for sports programs for disadvantaged kids. I am on three other boards, including one associated with my profession, and I also serve on the Advisory Council of the University of San Francisco's Graduate School of Business. My wife and I have made lots of new friends and have rekindled some old friendships. We also continue to travel often, spending time at our second home at Lake Tahoe and also spending a month a year in France.

Alan has had a very successful psychotherapy practice in New York for more than twenty-five years, specializing in relationships, career counseling, and life transitions. Alan has already begun to restructure his own life gradually by reorganizing his practice so that he now works four days a week instead of five and takes two months off in the summer. He is also starting a new phase of his practice, using the Birkman® personality profile with companies to allow them to make the very best use of their employees by structuring the job responsibilities around the interests and skills of the employees rather than the other way around. The goal is to create a "win-win-win" situation for the employees, the company, and its customers. Initial results are very encouraging.

In his practice, Alan has counseled many individuals who have not successfully made the transition to retirement. Because Alan's practice is in New York City, many of these individuals are high-net-worth, successful people who retired with more than enough money. But, soon after retiring, these people found that their lives did not get better—but got worse! Without the need to go to work every day, they lost the structure and purpose in their lives, they missed their friends at work, and their relationships with their family and spouse deteriorated. They lost direction, became frustrated, and felt adrift. Having prepared well for a successful career, they had not prepared adequately for what came afterward, and now they were "failing" their retirement and paying the price.

This is not surprising, when you think about it. Research has consistently shown that people who "hang it up" at the standard retirement age of sixty-two or sixty-five and who cease to contribute and be productive and active die earlier than those who continue to engage fully in society. In contrast, those who remain active, maintain a good weight and diet, and continue to engage in society and learn new things are less likely to have high blood pressure, high cholesterol, Alzheimer's, dementia, and other traditional old-age health problems. The lesson is clear and simple: living life to the fullest extends it. As a result, you can live like you are in your fifties well into your seventies and sometimes eighties.

An excellent book on this subject is *Younger Next Year* by Chris Crowley and Henry S. Lodge, M.D. It is a good companion piece to read with this book. After all, as Eleanor Roosevelt said, "When you cease to make a contribution, you begin to die." And George Burns, approaching his ninety-eighth birthday, said, "How can I die? I'm booked!"

Another French Paradox

Comparing American society with France can provide some cultural perspectives on retirement. While living in France, I learned that the French like to bring structure to everything. Consequently, for better or worse, they live in a very structured society.

It is not surprising, then, that the French also think about life in a very structured way. For them, life divides itself into three stages, or "âges." *Le premier âge* begins at birth and continues through the end of formal education. This period is, from a societal point of view, formative and nonproductive. *Le deux-ième âge* encompasses the productive work years, including raising a family, which is a very productive period because it both creates value and also guarantees the continuation of the race. *Le troisiàme âge* is "la retraite," the retreat from society, or retirement, which is funded primarily by the government.

It still works that way in France. But it no longer works that way in America. In our much less structured and more entrepreneurial society, it doesn't have to. And it shouldn't!

Society loses when potentially productive people leave the workforce. Although some of us work in professions requiring intense physical labor, most of us make our living with our minds, and "a mind is a terrible thing to waste," regardless of race or age. Not to mention society's loss of the older worker's wealth of experience. While retirement in France brings financial security, retired French people have less ability to continue to contribute, which is not good either for them or for their country.

Why do the French and other European societies do it this way? Because they believe that older people need to move on to make positions available for younger people coming into the workforce. In a more expansionary society like ours, that is not necessary, and—even if it were—contributions to society can come from activities other than work.

In America, perhaps more than in other Western countries, we work harder, take fewer vacations, and sacrifice many of our other life goals and ambitions for our careers. Retirement, finally, is our chance to pursue some of those "other things" we always wanted to do. But how do we make the right decisions that will lead to a balanced and fulfilling third chapter in our lives?

Troubled Transitions

Many do not succeed in the transition to retirement. For example, Ron, who was a career civil servant with the federal government, took his standard retirement package at age sixty-five. He and his wife, Muriel, sold their three-bedroom house in New Jersey and moved to a condo in Tampa. "We always wanted to retire to Florida, to get out of the rat race and the lousy weather. Every winter, we spent two wonderful weeks there. But after a year sitting on the beach and playing golf, we found that we missed our friends back home, I missed my colleagues at work, I missed being productive, we both missed the cultural attractions of the city, we missed our kids who were busy with their own lives, and there we sat, looking at the ocean, bored silly and realizing we had made a big mistake. Those things we always thought we wanted were not what we really wanted at all."

Ron and Muriel eventually moved back to New Jersey, but housing prices had risen in their absence, and they found themselves in weaker financial circumstances than before. "We made a big mistake," Ron says. "If only we had rented in Florida and tried out a year there first, we would now be so much better off."

Another example is William, who was a Wall Street professional, very successful financially, and who had always dreamed of being an actor. He "retired." Finally, he had the time and the money to pursue his dream. But after having been a "master of the universe" for thirty years, he found that having people half his age criticizing his acting abilities and stage performance skills was difficult for him. Uncharacteristically, he began to have self-doubts. Maybe he was not as good an actor as he thought. Maybe he was not prepared to start all over again in another profession for which he had neither adequately trained nor prepared.

Fortunately, this story has a happy ending. Based on a former colleague's suggestion, William decided to get some professional life coaching, which gave him access to many of the same techniques you will read about in later chapters of this book. After better understanding his own interests, skills, and needs, he decided to quit acting and instead become a part-time producer of off-Broadway shows. Now he is expending his energy in productive, creative, and mean-ingful ways in his new chosen field, and he loves his new life.

The question is how do you know enough about yourself and your prospective plans to avoid making the wrong decisions?

You prepare, that's how. Just like you prepared before. *Your Retirement, Your Way* will take you through the process and give you all the tools you need.

How You Will Create Your Master Plan

To create your personal, customized NewLife Master Plan, we will lead you through a structured process that will give you the power to take your future life into your own hands and create the best possible retirement lifestyle unique to your own interests, personality, relationships, and situation.

Knowing yourself and evaluating the possibilities in a meaningful way is the first part of this book.

The second part is making it happen, which involves personal strategic planning. Professionals who provide advice and guidance in late-career transitions know from experience that, for most people, a full-time, brand-new second career is not the optimal solution. Rather, they advise their clients to begin planning strategically for the next stage of their new life, including setting personal goals for where they hope to be, such as what they hope to achieve and by when. This involves setting realistic goals, then periodically measuring progress toward them. If you have given yourself a year to learn to play your favorite Mozart sonatas on the piano, and, at the end of that year, you have still not mastered "Chopsticks," hey, it's not working, my friend. Revise the plan. Make a change. You are seeking happiness and fulfillment, not endless frustration.

You were very proactive in preparing for your career. Now you can be proactive in preparing for what we call your NewLife. If you do it right, these later years can be the happiest and most inspiring of all, providing you with the opportunity to explore and develop those parts of yourself that were previously dormant, while continuing to use many of the skills you already have. Creating your customized NewLife Master Plan is a proactive approach to evaluating and then systematically expanding the opportunities in life that still await you.

Two Authors, Two Voices

As you will see from taking the mini-Birkman® in Chapter 4, personality types are classified into colors: Red, Blue, Yellow, and Green. In his chapters, Alan speaks more in the Blue voice and represents personality types who are more contemplative and introspective. The Blues are Type B personalities who take their time, like to analyze every move carefully, and hesitate to embrace rapid or total change. These can be good traits in retirement planning, if used correctly, but they also can be barriers to moving forward with your NewLife. I, on the other hand, in my chapters, speak in the Red voice (which, in my case, also spills over into the Green) and represent personalities who are predominantly self-directed, take-charge, Type A persuasive types who think that they know exactly what they want and how to get it. This can be good, too, except that without sufficient self-analysis and introspection, the destination can be wrong and the results can be disastrous as the previous examples illustrate.

There is no one right answer for everyone. We are all unique personalities, with some combinations of the Birkman® colors. The purpose of this book is not to change your personality but to help you better understand it and yourself so that you can make the right choices for your NewLife in retirement.

How to Get the Most Out of This Book

Before getting started, here are four suggestions to help you get the most out of this book:

1. **Don't speed read.**   If you take a week or a month or even longer to get through it, that's fine. It's probably better. You are creating the basis for your future life and happiness. What could be worth more quality time and thought than that?
2. **Read each chapter in its proper sequence.**   Creating your NewLife Master Plan is a "building block" process. You have to do the self-analysis exercises before you start creating your NewLife plans. Jumping ahead won't work because you will not have the information you will need to do it right. A good foundation is essential to building a sound structure.

3. **Engage.**   This is your life. Have confidence in your ability to change it and create the future you have long dreamed about. Retirement in our culture is a do-it-yourself process, and this book was written to help you do it to the best of your ability.

4. **Write down your answers.**   Avoid the common reluctance to write in books.* This book is a workbook, and it is just for you. You don't need to share it, lend it, or give it to anybody. You can't just think about how you would answer the questions in the abstract. You have to sharpen your pencil, think though the questions, and write down your best answers in the spaces provided. Later on, you will be asked to return to what you have written to create your NewLife Master Plan Summary. If you have not written it down, it won't work, and trying to reconstruct your earlier thoughts will be inefficient and frustrating. We can help you interpret the results of the tests and exercises, but you have to do the work. You are investing the time in your future, and the return on your investment will be substantial. Destroy this book to save your future!

---

*If you can't, then photocopy the pages that require a response and write your answers there.

2

Preparing Psychologically for Change

Alan Bernstein

There must be an ending before there can be a beginning.

—WILLIAM BRIDGES, SPEAKER, AUTHOR

The Psychotherapist's Perspective

Unlike my friend and writing partner, John, my style is to consider carefully all options before I make a move. At my best, I am a cautious and thoughtful soul who ponders change with intensity. (For example, when I started to use a computer, I first read a book about the history of computers before I turned mine on!) When I work with people in my practice as a psychotherapist, I encourage careful personal analysis, using both historical and current factors. I will be doing the same with you.

My personal style has great rewards—rarely do I lose a friend or client. The risk, however, is the possibility of getting stuck at the thought level—"analysis paralysis" as we call it in this book—rather than proceeding to the actions needed to get where we want to go. Thus, my partnership with John was conceived. I wanted an expert strategist, someone comfortable with motivating people to move into uncharted territory. We could be the Lewis and Clark of retirement planning, with me scouting the territory of psychological motivation and John leading the troops over the unexplored passes! I tell you this because, like all authors, we wish to explore the hidden recesses of our interests and expand our capabilities. John, I am happy to report, understands that people who wander about in their thought style are not necessarily wasting time. They simply process differently.

The Birkman® Personality Profile

Your Retirement, Your Way will teach you how to highlight your primary needs, both conscious and preconscious, as you make your choices for the future. It will also help you to compare your interpretation of your own history with a database of more than 1.5 million people who have contributed to the Birkman® archives by using a personality profile that you will fill out in Chapter 4. You will thus be using state-of-the art tools to reveal your personal interests, working style, and motivational needs, and you will then be able to leverage these powerful tools as you go about the business of applying them in your chosen NewLife.

Once you have created your mini-Birkman® personality profile, you will have two vantage points, coded by color, from which to contemplate your personality. One color will be your interests, and the other color will combine your style and motivational needs. The tension between these two colors will largely describe your personality.

In addition to the Birkman® personality profile, you have at your disposal another tool that will help you chart your course: your memory. By looking back to look forward, you will be able to see who you were and better assess who you want to become. In Chapter 3, I will be your guide as you reflect on the experiences that made you *you*. The exercises you will find there are designed to illuminate those times in your life when your energy level was at its highest. What were you doing? What was the environment you enjoyed working in? What were your motivations at the time? By excavating these moments—as well as their underlying causes—you will be able to pinpoint the common denominators needed to achieve what Mihaly Csikszentmihalyi refers to as a state of "flow" in his book *Flow: The Psychology of Optimal Experience.*

Each of us has experienced this phenomenon over the course of our life. A state of flow occurs when you "lose" yourself in a project or activity, when what you are doing is so absorbing that linear time vanishes. It is when you feel most fulfilled.

The purpose of sifting through this preconscious information will be to recreate this state of flow as you approach your retirement. Reading on, you will discover what energizes you, what motivates you, and how to apply these to your NewLife. Your subjective memory analysis, coupled with the objective results of the Birkman® personality profile, will provide you with a balanced look at who you are and how to be your best self going forward.

It really is a package deal. We have found that the synergy created between the memory analysis and the Birkman® imparts a powerful psychological traction that will help you navigate the future. With these tools at your fingertips, you will discover the factors and situations that motivated you in the past and gain the confidence to now repeat the performance.

Key Motivators in Your Personality

The tools of retirement planning answer a real need. You may feel ambivalent or resistant to a change of this magnitude. After all, you are not just starting a new job or buying a new home. You are embarking on a new way of living. The enormity of the choice to retire should not be discounted. At the same time, however, giving in to your apprehension will only delay your satisfaction and happiness.

Let this book be a safe haven in which you can address these fears. As you work through the lessons and tools in the following chapters, you will have the opportunity to step back and consider how you can best confront change. Use this time to decide what elements of yourself you want to take with you into your NewLife and what elements you want to leave behind. Change on this level requires vitality, strength, and the trust that, once you are on the other side, you will still be recognizable to yourself.

Of course, you will encounter internal roadblocks along the way. Fear of change and analysis paralysis are both common hindrances that can prevent you from moving forward. How can you break free of the fears that keep you rooted in place?

Inertia is no more powerful a force in the physical world than in your emotional one. Just as it takes more energy to stop a train than to let it keep rolling, putting the brakes on the life you know and with which you are now comfortable will take some effort. In your present life, you more or less know what each day will bring. The security of your daily routines feels safe; you are at ease with it, and you know the role that you play. Keep in mind, though, that there is a danger to the comfort you feel in your daily routines: it prevents you from truly embracing the opportunities that await you.

To retire with a sense of pleasure and purpose, you need to realize that, whatever anxieties come along with making this change, you are still in control of your own destiny.

By choosing to retire, you are making a strong and vibrant decision to choose opportunity over security. Think of all of the times in your life that you've decided to take a chance. In retrospect, are you glad you made the decisions that pushed you to try something new? Although difficult at the time, you can probably now see how those challenges allowed you to learn and grow. Likewise, choosing to retire is the ultimate opportunity for personal growth.

As you read *Your Retirement, Your Way,* you will learn to devise ways in which to navigate emotionally the transition into retirement. In my experience, both personally and professionally, it takes an enormous amount of emotional strength to defy and overcome the anxiety of the unknown. On any given day, you may feel sad, paralyzed, fearful, or just plain cranky. These are emotional states that will come and go during this transition. Don't overthink a bad day. Do pay attention to the overall pattern of your moods. (If you feel sad or anxious the majority of the time, you may need to change your current path.) By helping you generate psychological energy for change, this process will give you the tools to understand and manage your emotional states.

When it comes to retiring, people have a diverse range of experience—on both an emotional and practical level. However, the Birkman® personality profile and the search for the state of flow as well as the other exercises in this book will shine a bright light on how your *specific* personality can best cope with change. What do you like to do? How do you best communicate? How do you handle conflict? The answers to these questions and many others will draw a picture of what motivates you. At that point, the "unknown" will start looking less like a mystery and more like an opportunity.

The Ultimate Goal

I will be your companion as you contemplate the dangers ahead—What if I make a mistake? What if I don't like my choices? What if I don't have enough money?—while John will be reminding you that you can always correct your course and that the worst danger is doing nothing! My deepest wish is that, by analyzing and understanding your key motivators and through the precision and intelligence of John's strategies, you will gain the psychological thrust and energy you need to choose a direction for your NewLife, understand its value, articulate its aim, and then create an action plan and timetable to help you realize your goals. The ultimate goal, of course, is happiness and fulfillment in retirement, which will come from creating a life that is thoughtfully and personally designed by you and for you alone.

The exploration begins in Chapter 3.

3

Who Were You? Who Are You? Who Can You Become?

Alan Bernstein

Tell me what you love, and I'll tell you who you are.

—ATTRIBUTION UNKNOWN

I have but one lamp by which my feet are guided, and that is the lamp of experience.

—PATRICK HENRY, LAWYER, POLITICIAN, REVOLUTIONARY WAR HERO

Before planning your future, it is first necessary to examine your past to answer some very important questions. What parts of your full-time career and nonwork life will you want to transfer to your NewLife? What elements of them will you gladly leave behind? Who are you now? What makes you tick? What do you really enjoy? What really gives you satisfaction? Voyages into your past can offer surprising insights in answering these questions. We have all processed memories that contain information about our most passionate interests, in what environment or style we enjoy doing them, and what inner motivators or needs are being met when we are at the top of our game. You can train yourself to tap into this wellspring of intuition through close observation and careful thought. The remembrance of things past is the most tantalizing part of your retirement planning process because it often yields telling, preconscious information you might otherwise overlook but that can reinforce the foundation of your overall retirement plan.

The exercises in this chapter require intense concentration, the kind you need when you prepare a complicated recipe, conduct research on the Internet, compose a memo to your boss or an important client, or study for an exam. Still, to help you interpret your postretirement needs and interests, your assignment is simple, yet with complex meanings. You will be asked to remember isolated incidents in which you accomplished tasks you weren't sure you could do, yet that were so absorbing that time slipped away. You were in a state of flow, and ordinary linear time disappeared.

Your Satisfaction Highlights

Who were you when you were at your best? Your past "flow states" provide pivotal clues about what generally makes you feel fulfilled. To get started, think back to those environments or situations in which you've been most creative. They can be from school, work, the PTA, hobbies, your book club, playing with your kids—wherever you've felt that you were completely satisfied to be doing what you were doing in the way you were doing it. Try to come up with ten such situations.

What I Was Doing When I Was at My Best

1. _Knowledgeable abt my job +_
proficient in drug in

2. _Well-respected by peers_

3. _Part of group + valued co-worker_

4.

5. _____

_____

_____

_____

_____

6. _____

_____

_____

_____

_____

7. _____

_____

_____

_____

_____

8. _____

_____

_____

_____

_____

9. _____

_____

_____

_____

_____

_____

10. _____

_____

_____

_____

_____

Stumped? For many of us, identifying the happiest times of our lives can be a daunting task. How to choose? Which ones merit noting? To get you started, here's one example from Sharon, a sixty-three-year-old former hospital fund-raising/development executive turned full-time "retired" farmer. Sharon came to see me because she felt that her retirement plan was "imbalanced." Farming full time provided lots of fresh air and exercise (definite plusses), but it was isolating and not necessarily intellectually stimulating. "I often have days in which I feel like I want to do something new and different," she told me. Clearly, her self-styled "retirement" plan needed tweaking—but how? No doubt, Sharon had the answers locked up in a lifetime of experience. Her first step toward discovering them was to start writing. Here are six situations that she penned:

1. *I'm happiest when I complete a project in which the end result is something constructive—a positive end product, such as raising more than $1 million one year for the hospital's radiology department. It was so gratifying to see the x-ray equipment up and running, knowing that I helped make it happen.*
2. *I enjoy volunteering for the local Kiwanis Club in my town and with the hospital auxiliary.*
3. *I enjoyed years of working with my young family. I had a balanced life that wasn't so much focused on work.*
4. *I enjoy working outside, gardening, etc. There's a part of me that enjoys working with my hands.*
5. *I enjoyed attending classes for my Masters in Public Administration.*
6. *I enjoy "facilitating" and organizing the affairs of my elderly family members.*

If you haven't filled out ten happiness highlights, do it now. Or proceed to the next exercise, which may jog your memory.

Your Worst Memories

If you are a critical thinker, conjuring up your happiest memories may be especially challenging. Instead, try this exercise as a reverse twist to jog your memories.

Situations in Which I've Been at My Worst

1. When I didn't know what was expected of me or I didn't know how to do something and had to ask for help

2. Conflictual interactions when others angry n resentful.

3. Working w/o purpose or sense of direction, Like being productive.

4. _____

   _____

   _____

   _____

   _____

   _____

5. _____

   _____

   _____

   _____

   _____

   _____

Take a moment to identify places and situations you'd describe as your life's low points. As an example, we've had clients describe crying at work, being ridiculed by a boss, working full-time after just having had twins, or pulling an all-nighter to meet a deadline. Of her worst memories, as an example, Sharon simply wrote, "Working with a CEO I didn't see eye to eye with and sitting in meetings in which nothing happened—a waste of time."

Why dredge up the negative? Because your valleys can be as informative as your peaks. The purpose of this second list is to help you work by default—to examine what absences or situations in your life created bad feelings, whether physical or psychological. You may then be able to work backward to create your list of what conditions encourage you to feel happy and creative (your satisfaction highlights).

Looking at the list of "worst" experiences you've written about, what was it about these particular situations that made your life hell? Was it the people you were working with? The assigned task? The lack of control? The conditions you were working under? Write your thoughts here.

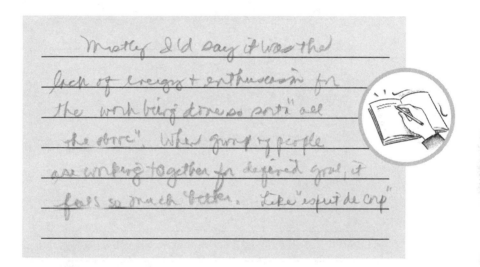

Your "Flow" Chart

After you've finished your happiness list, select at least five specific memories from that list when you were so involved in a project, accomplishing a task, or solving a problem that you can recall the sense of ordinary linear time slipping away, such that you couldn't tell how long you'd been working. Take a moment now to list them here. They'll be core events about which you'll construct key stories later on.

My Selected Flow Memories

1. _figuring out math n logic_
   problems. Felt so good to
   accomplish a difficult mental
   challenge!

   _____

2. _____

   _____

   _____

   _____

   _____

3. _____

   _____

   _____

   _____

   _____

4. _____

   _____

   _____

   _____

   _____

5. _____

_____

_____

_____

_____

Now, reorder these memories subjectively, placing the ones you remember with the most pride or pleasure at the top. Then write a story about your number-one memory. What happened? Be specific; appeal to the senses. What did it feel like to be there? Were there colors, odors, textures? What were you doing? What were you trying to accomplish? Did you expect to be able to do it? Who were you with? Was it necessary that they were there? How long did you expect it to take? How good did you think it would be when you were done? Try to answer these questions in detail. Imagine yourself at a retirement-planning seminar, reading the story to a group of your peers who are sitting on the edge of their seats, wondering what happened next. What were the results? Write your story in a separate notebook.

Paul's Story

As an example, here's the story that Paul, a fifty-eight-year-old pediatrician who was contemplating retirement, wrote about buying and repairing his first car.

> When I first bought a car in my early twenties, a used Peugeot 403, I was totally intimidated by the task of having to

care for it. In my high school years, I had secretly borrowed the family car one night and blown its engine as, unknown to me, it had an oil leak. Needless to say, the idea of caring for a foreign car (this was 1964) seemed both overwhelming and exotic. Moreover, the head of its engine needed to be rebuilt. I had a friend who was an engineer and a creative type, a rare combination in those days, and he agreed to help me tackle the task. One late afternoon, we started on the project, continuing well into the evening by the glow of flashlight and oil lamp. I was exhilarated to be actually working on a technical, mechanical project and not ruining or breaking it but fixing it. I was the only one in my immediate family with any interest in or inclination toward mechanics. In fact, my family lived in a rented apartment in New York City. We called the handyman to change a light bulb. So, to me, the notion of mechanically caring for something as complex as an automobile was tremendously exciting and almost frightening. I felt I was perhaps transcending some inherited, even genetic barrier by loosening screws in an orderly manner and uncoupling things from one another in such a way that they could be healed.

From this story, you might think that Paul was mechanically inclined and that putting things together and taking them apart were his "thing." Well, you'd be partially right. He revealed that he worked in a bicycle shop during his junior and senior years of college, but his passion wasn't really for mechanics—after all, he became a physician. What were his interests? What kinds of things did he gravitate toward that might serve him well in retirement? Well, clearly there was a car, there was the support of friendship, and there was the negotiating and purchasing of items, not to mention organizing the project. One of the ways we find meaning in our personal stories is to orient ourselves to see what active behaviors we're actually drawn to and what style we have when we're working at our best. In this case, Paul concluded that the following actions and skills made this experience so meaningful for him that he might import them into his retirement.

- Working with his hands
- Solving a problem
- Sharing the experience
- Completing the project
- Being his own boss
- Taking a risk, knowing that the project could fail, but that he could make it succeed
- Negotiating to buy the car
- Learning to maintain the car
- Selecting a mentor
- Persisting in figuring out how to care for the car
- Dedicating himself to a project
- Researching and organizing the project
- Developing physical dexterity to use the tools
- Venturing outside his comfort zone
- Freeing himself from preconceived notions
- Not being discouraged by his previous error
- Presuming that he could be better than he thought

Perhaps the most subtle and yet most important elements of the story are how Paul's needs were met. After thinking it over, Paul concluded, "I think I needed to take on a project that was bigger than what I was comfortable with and complete it. I also wanted to explore an area with which I was totally unfamiliar. I also liked the idea of taking things apart and putting them back together so that they came together better."

Sharon's Story

To practice your skills at interpreting memories and mining them for personal insight, we invite you to take a stab at one of Sharon's flow memories. At the end of the following story, list the actions or skills she used, then put an asterisk next to those that seem, from the context of her vignette, especially meaningful to her.

> A couple of years ago, I received a phone call from an attorney for my Aunt Ester. He indicated that Ester was no longer able to handle her affairs and that I should become her guardian/conservator. Because Ester was incapacitated, I'd need to be court appointed. After discussion with family members, I took on that job. The part of this project that was intense for me was when I had to sell Aunt Ester's home and dispose of her possessions because she was moving to a nursing home. The will she had prepared years earlier indicated that the one thing she didn't want was to have her assets sold at an auction or garage sale. So I contacted all of her relatives and set up a time when they could come and pick out items they would like. That was a good day because I got to see long-lost relatives and I got the house cleaned out. The house was listed with a real estate agent and sold in one day. All this took about a month, but it seemed like something was always happening and time flew.

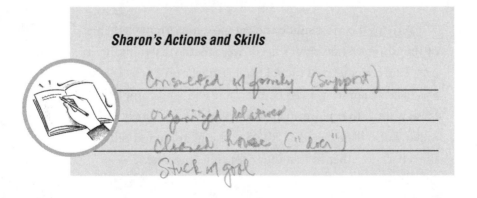

Sharon's Actions and Skills

Consulted w/ family (support)

organized relatives

Cleaned house ("doa")

Stuck to goal

_____

_____

_____

_____

Setting Out on Your Inner Journey

Now, it's your turn. From your story about your number-one memory, take a minute to list the actions or skills you used when you were at your best. Then put an asterisk next to those you think helped make the experience meaningful.

_____

_____

_____

_____

_____

_____

Interpreting Your Story

At this juncture, we're going to go even deeper into your pre-conscious and isolate the motivators, the needs, the key intangibles from your past that gave you a feeling of deep satisfaction. Have your pen handy. We're going to take it step by step.

1. Your Interests

Again, read your story to yourself. Note what you did, what you were drawn to, what the action or subject is—in short, your interests. These are the things you're interested in, what you like to do. They also tell you what your goals are or what you're trying to achieve. In Paul's story, his interest was fixing a car. What interests were revealed in your story?

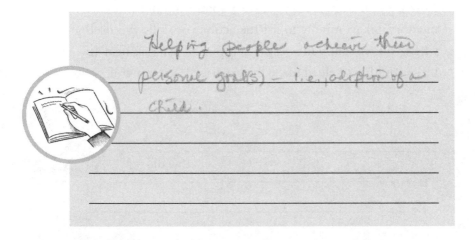

_____ Helping people achieve their
_____ personal goal(s) — i.e., adoption of a
_____ child.

2. Your Style

Next, observe your style, the manner in which you operated in this memory. Were you alone, with one other person, or in a group? If you were in a group, were you leading or following? Your usual style of behavior assumes that all of your personal and psychological needs are being met. Style can also be described in the following ways. Circle all that apply to you in your selected memory.

- Having plenty to do ✓
- Having to make clear-cut decisions
- Having others be direct and logical ✓
- Having objective supervision ✓
- Knowing exactly what to do ✓
- Being able to work without interruption
- Getting low-key direction
- Being trusted ✓
- Having others be democratic ✓
- Using a variety of skills
- Having others encourage competition
- Enjoying novelty and variety of work
- Having others encourage feelings ✓
- Feeling free from constant social demands
- Having a self-determined schedule
- Enjoying individualized rewards
- Knowing who is in charge ✓

Now, make a note of your own style. How did you carry out the actions in your story?

Knew role, self - directed, trusted
by others, accomplished task

3. Your Needs

What needs did you find gratifying or satisfying from your memory? Circle those that apply.

- Did you demonstrate independence?
- Did you contribute to a feeling of community?
- Were you working alone? With one other person? With a group?
- Were you working for self-gain?
- Were you working to be important to others?
- Were you working for philosophical or altruistic purposes?
- Were you working for yourself? For someone else? For an organization?
- Were you directing and controlling the situation?
- Were you playing an indispensable role?
- Were you carrying out orders?
- Were you directing others?
- Were you helping others?
- Were you learning something new?
- Were you being creative?
- Were you influencing others?

Now make your own needs notes about what conditions were present and satisfied in your story of your number-one memory.

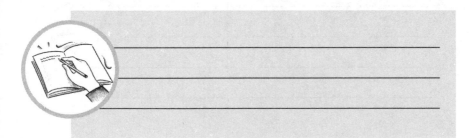

If you find it difficult to answer the needs question, you may find that operating from stress, when your needs were not being met, is easier. To get a general idea of the needs that were being met for you in your selected memory, work backward by answering the following general questions:

How do I behave when many of my needs are not being met?

_____

_____

_____

_____

In which environment (people, place, stress levels) am I least productive?

People I work worst with:

_____ Bossy, dogmatic "overtalkers" who _____

_____ never get off the dime. Backstabbers _____

_____

Place(s) I can't stand:

_____ Busy, noisy, chaotic places _____

_____

_____

Stress level: I do my worst work when I'm:

Pushed to do something fast

Don't have clear direction

Overall, I work best in the following circumstances:

Clear purpose, supportive

environment, ample time

4. Your Skills

After you've defined your favorite interests, the style in which you prefer to pursue them, and the needs you must meet to operate at your most creative level, isolate the skills you used over the course of your story. Skills are the abilities and resources that you would bring to a retirement situation. In your story, what skills were revealed?

Why do I think I chose this story?

_____

_____

_____

_____

Applying Memories: Carol's Story

To help you interpret your memories, examples are often helpful. Here's one written by Carol, a marketing executive in her midfifties who attended a retirement-planning seminar we conducted. She gave her memory a title: "Amelia's coat."

It's safe to say that 1982 wasn't a good year for my husband, George, and me. We had started the year with the news that Amelia, our eighteen-month-old daughter, would need open-heart surgery. Then, I discovered I was pregnant again, which was unexpected. Finally, George learned he hadn't made partner at Coopers. It was August, and he was away on a three-week life-planning course. It was hot and muggy, and I was lonely. I should have gone away to visit my family, but George's departure was last minute, and I was gripped in a torpid moment. Typically in August, I begin to lust for cooler, autumnal weather. I decided to make Amelia a plaid car coat and took out a lovely plaid woolen fabric I had been saving and decided to make the coat reversible in matching blue wool I also had. Years ago, I had made a plaid coat for myself, which I thought turned out well, though not perfect because the lining didn't sit well in the lower hem and I never could bring myself to add buttons and buttonholes. So I'd had some practice but still went slowly, carefully following instructions as I have now learned to do in sewing and not cutting corners to save time.

Basting and ironing are the two most important aspects of sewing. I purposely made the coat big so it would last several years and also made a matching skirt. It's my finest work to date with perfect matching at all the seams. When Amelia wore it, it made her look unique—which she is—and I felt proud to say I made it. I took a picture and sent it to my mother, who had taught me to sew, so she could enjoy my success also. Even George has told others I made it.

To help Carol interpret this memory, we began by exploring her interests by asking her what drew her to this project. A sense of fashion? Her enjoyment in self-education ("carefully following instructions and not cutting corners to save time")? Her desire to complete unfinished projects? ("Years ago, I had made . . . turned out well, though not perfect . . .") While she contemplated this question, Carol made the following observations about her style in this particular story:

- "I enjoyed converting feelings into artistry."
- "I like working with my hands."
- "I tend to be meticulous."

We also pointed out that:

- She showed perseverance and demonstrated an ability to express and transmit her experience.
- When challenged, she eventually becomes active ("in a torpid moment . . . I decided to make . . .").
- Though her feelings impel her toward paralyzing responses ("I should have gone away . . . I was gripped"), her aesthetic and pragmatic responses are her deeper needs ("I decided to make . . . carefully following instructions . . . and not cutting corners").

- Ultimately, she generates self-respect through her achievement ("It's my finest work . . . I feel so proud . . .").

How could you use this in-depth information about yourself? Put your story under a similar microscope. Note the actions you used in your story. (In our example, we'd note Carol's hand-eye skills [sewing, ironing] and her ability to learn by carefully following instructions.) Then ask yourself: What made me feel rewarded? What needs of mine were being met?

In Carol's case:

- She found an active way to feel close to her mother, her daughter, and her husband through an achievement.
- She was able to transform strong feeling into an aesthetic shape ("I was gripped" and "I begin to lust for" became the creative wellspring for "I decided," "I had been saving" and "I settled on" and are eventually transformed into "a reversible coat" with "perfect matching at all the seams").
- She was methodical and skilled in using resources she had.
- She was focused, decisive, resourceful, and creatively self-challenging in response to a "bad . . . year" (her daughter's surgery, an unplanned pregnancy, and her husband's three-week absence and uncertain professional future).

Summarizing Your Story

You should now have a better idea of your interests, your style, your needs, and your skills. You also should have a better understanding of the situations and environments in which you flourish. Take a moment to prepare your own summary here.

My Interests:

Helping others toward goals

Using my knowledge and skills to
       help others & feel useful in process

Contributing to well-being of others

Being needed in productive pursuit

My Style:

Having plenty to do

Objective, knowledgeable supervision

Knowing what to do

Need to be respected & trusted

Clear expectations

My Needs:

Some direction but also some freedom

To be needed & respected

Good teamwork

Growth + continued learning

My Skills:

Assessment

Working w/ people

Able to write well

Diplomacy in dealing w/ others.

Situations/Environments in Which I Flourish:

Supportive, goal-oriented environment
Need some freedom to try new

ideas

Keep this summary in mind as we move into Chapter 4, in which we will use the Birkman® personality profile to examine your personality in even greater depth.

What Color Is Your Retirement?

Alan Bernstein

To thyne own self be true.

—WILLIAM SHAKESPEARE,
POET, PLAYWRIGHT

I n my psychotherapy practice, I regularly use the Birk-man®* personality profile to better understand people negotiating complex transitions. It is not a clinical psychological assessment but instead profiles the behavior of normal, functioning people. The Birkman® makes clear our areas of interest and our need to operate at our best, even when we are under stress. It builds on the memories analysis of the previous chapter and provides both a window into the motivational needs that lie beneath our actions and a way to understand the layers of our personalities.

---

*The Birkman® information presented herein is the exclusive property of Birkman International, Inc., and was adapted with the special limited permission of Birkman International, Inc. All rights reserved by and to Birkman International, Inc.

This chapter offers an opportunity to develop and deepen the intuitive leaps you made in Chapter 3. This customized, brief version of the Birkman® profile is a profound instrument packed in a miniature gift box. You will be able to affirm or modify what the memories you recalled in the preceding chapter have already stimulated: knowledge of your interests and the style in which you like to accomplish or pursue your activities. For example, two people may enjoy going to the gym to work out during their time off. One may enjoy the solitariness of weight lifting while the other enjoys a pick-up basketball game. For both, the time represents an opportunity to work out, of course, but the basketball game may appeal to the competitive nature of one, while the other may be refreshed by the meditative quality of his weight-lifting ritual.

Again, bear in mind that this is a brief version of the Birkman® personality profile. If you wish to pursue the full spectrum of insight that the full profile can provide, you can contact Birkman® online at birkman.com to schedule a full profile and be debriefed by a consultant. However, you can use this brief version to introduce yourself to the concept and to help you discover in-depth information about your personality that will help you assess your interests as well as your style. It will also give you insight into what does *not* motivate you.

This version of the Birkman® profile is a simple way to visualize your overall behavior. The following questions are a condensed and self-scored version of The Birkman Method® created especially for this book. As I mentioned in the previous chapter, this profile allows you to gain access to broad information about yourself. The questions presented here use The Birkman Method® research material and enable you to apply it to clarify both your interests (symbolized by "I") and your style (symbolized by "S"). This will be a major asset in defining not only *what* you are drawn to, but also *how* you like to achieve your goals.

The Life Style Grid®

The Birkman® Interest and Style Summary plots aspects of your personality and behavior on a grid with four quadrants, each identified by a color.

The Life Style Grid® is based on a model of how people behave in general, and this particular model has been used for thousands of years. The first person to use it was probably Hippocrates, the "father of medicine"; in fact, the grid is sometimes called the *Hippocratic Model*. Hippocrates claimed that he could take all of the people in the world, divide them into four categories, and accurately describe how they would act or behave. According to Hippocrates, there are four basic temperaments—Implementers, Communicators, Planners, and Administrators—and he bases his model on this idea. Models or pictures are not perfect; they are only generalizations. This one, however, is a very good generalization of how most people behave most of the time.

The Grid Symbols

There are two aspects of your personality and behavior that will appear on this grid:

(I)   An "I" indicates your retirement interests, what you want to do, as indicated by your interest patterns. In other words, it shows the type of results you want and the kind of activities that will give you the most satisfaction. This does not measure skill or ability around those interests, only preference. The color location of your "I" suggests what you like to do.

The Life Style Grid®

Outgoing (Exerts direct authority)

<table>
<tr>
<td>

Red Implementers

Task oriented
Organizer
Delegates
Acts direct
Feels direct

</td>
<td>

Green Communicators

People oriented
Director
Works with people
  to get results
Acts direct
Feels sensitive

</td>
</tr>
<tr>
<td>

Yellow Administrators

Systems oriented
Controller
Uses systems to
  get results
Acts sensitive
Feels direct

</td>
<td>

Blue Planners

Idea oriented
Planner
Uses ideas to get
  results
Acts sensitive
Feels sensitive

</td>
</tr>
</table>

Factual (Objective) — Feelings (Subjective)

Reserved (Exerts indirect authority)   ™

(S)   An "S" indicates your style, how you like to do things or what your usual behavior is. The "S" describes your style, or active behavior, for pursuing your interests. This is your preferred mode of achieving your personal goals and is descriptive of the way in which you like to operate when all of your needs are met. It is how people see you acting most of the time. It is how you do things when everything is going your way. If your style color results feel antithetical to your real-life style, consider whether you are operating under stress on a day-to-day basis and remember that when considering your score. Your style is a complex symbol as it combines the external style (as someone watching you would describe your activity) along with internal hints about what best motivates you. If we explore our basketball player above, his interest is in sports and his style is likely competitive and oriented toward results. He may have Red interests and a Red style. However, if his motivation is to be a team member who can continue to set up shots for others and rejoice when the team wins, as opposed to how well he does individually, we may have someone with a Blue style, as his motivation is more related to the feeling of being part of a community.

As you fill in your mini-Birkman®, be thoughtful about the nuances of the symbols and how they reflect your memories in Chapter 3, as this profile can reflect many facets of your personality.

Now, please take the Birkman® Interest and Style Summary. After the summary, you will want to put your interest symbol (I) and your style symbol (S) in your Lifestyle Grid®.

The Birkman® Interest and Style Summary

To develop an estimate of your Birkman® colors for your interests and style, you will need to complete and self-score the following items. To do this, read each pair of phrases and decide which side of the pair is most descriptive of you, then put a check mark by that phrase.

Column A		*Column B*	
☑	1. I would rather be a wildlife expert.	I would rather be a public relations professional.	☐
☑	2. I would rather be a company controller.	I would rather be a TV news anchor.	☐
☐	3. I would rather be a tax lawyer.	I would rather be a newspaper editor.	☑
☐	4. I would rather be an auditor.	I would rather be a musician.	☑
☑	5. I would rather be a production manager.	I would rather be an advertising manager.	☐
☐	6. I would rather be an account- ing manager.	I would rather be a history professor.	☑
☑	7. I would rather be a bookkeeper.	I would rather be an electrician.	☐
☑	8. I would rather be a writer.	I would rather be an elected official.	☐
☐	9. I would rather be a clerical worker.	I would rather be a carpenter.	☑
☑	10. I would rather be a payroll manager.	I would rather be a manager of engineering.	☐
☐	11. I would rather be an audit manager.	I would rather be a safety manager.	☑
☑	12. I would rather be an artist.	I would rather be a salesperson.	☐
☑	13. I am usually patient when I have to wait for an appointment.	I get restless when I have to wait for an appointment.	☐
☐	14. It is easy to laugh at one's little social errors or faux pas.	It is hard to laugh at one's little social errors or faux pas.	☐
☑	15. It is wise to make it known if someone is doing some- thing that bothers you.	It is wise to remain silent if some- one is doing something that bothers you.	☐
☐	16. It's not really okay to argue with others even when you know you are right.	It's okay to argue with others when you know you are right.	☑
☑	17. I like to bargain to get a good price.	I don't like to have to bargain to get a good price.	☐
☐	18. It is easy to be outgoing and sociable at a party with strangers.	It is hard to be outgoing and sociable at a party with strangers.	☑

☑ 19. I would read the instructions first when putting together a new toy for a child. | I would just "jump in" and start putting together a new toy for a child. ☐

☑ 20. It is usually best to be pleasant and let others decide if your ideas are worth accepting. | It is usually best to be forceful and "sell" your ideas to others. ☐

☑ 21. I usually like to work cautiously. | I usually like to work fast. ☐

☑ 22. Generally I prefer to work quietly with a minimum of wasted movement. | Generally I prefer to move around and burn some energy while I work. ☐

☑ 23. I don't like to have to persuade others to accept my ideas when there is forceful opposition or argument from others. | I like to sell and promote my ideas with others even when it takes some argument. ☐

☑ 24. It is better to listen carefully and be sure you understand when topics are being discussed. | It is better to speak up quickly and be heard when topics are being discussed. ☐

Scoring Your Answers

Now that you have made your choices, you can score the list to determine the color of your interests and style. To accomplish this, you will need to count the number of items you marked in Column B and enter these counts in the following four spaces.

- First, count the number of items checked in Column B for the first six items (1–6) and write that count in this space: ___ (Interest H)
- Second, count the number of items checked in Column B for the second six items (7–12) and write that count in this space: ___ (Interest V)
- Third, count the number of items checked in Column B for the third six items (13–18) and write that count in this space: ___ (Style H)

- Fourth, count the number of items checked in Column B for the last six items (19–24) and write that count in this space: ___6___ (Style V)

Your Interest Color

Now that you have these four counts, estimate your interest and style colors. For interest, read the following four statements and see which one describes your counts. The color associated with the statement that is correct for your counts is the best *estimate* of your interest color.

- **Blue.** Your interest color is probably Blue if your Interest H count is 4 or more (4, 5, or 6) and your Interest V count is 3 or less (1, 2, or 3). You like creative, humanistic, thoughtful, and quiet types of responsibilities and professions.
- **Green.** Your interest color is probably Green if your Interest H count is 4 or more (4, 5, or 6) and your Interest V count is 4 or more (4, 5, or 6). You like persuasive, selling, promotional, and group-contact types of responsibilities and professions.
- **Red.** Your interest color is probably Red if your Interest H count is 3 or less (1, 2, or 3) and your Interest V count is 4 or more (4, 5, or 6). You like practical, technical, objective, hands-on, and problem-solving types of responsibilities and professions.
- **Yellow.** Your interest color is probably Yellow if your Interest H count is 3 or less (1, 2, or 3) and your Interest V count is 3 or less (1, 2, or 3). You like organized, detail-oriented, predictable, and objective types of responsibilities and professions.

Place an "I," indicating your retirement interests, in the appropriate color square of the blank Life Style Grid®.

The Life Style Grid®

Red	Green
Yellow " I " " S "	**Blue**

TM

Your Style Color

To estimate your style color, read the four statements below and see which one describes your counts for style. The color associated with the statement that is correct for your counts is the best estimate of your style color.

- **Blue.**   Your style color is probably Blue if your Style H count is 4 or more (4, 5, or 6) and your Style V count is

3 or less (1, 2, or 3). You prefer to perform your responsibilities in a manner that is supportive and helpful to others with a minimum of confrontation. You prefer to work where you and others have time to think things through before acting.

- **Green.**   Your style color is probably Green if your Style H count is 4 or more (4, 5, or 6) and your Style V count is 4 or more (4, 5, or 6). You prefer to perform your responsibilities in a manner that is outgoing and even forceful. You prefer to work where things get done with a minimum of thought and where persuasion is well received by others.
- **Red.**   Your style color is probably Red if your Style H count is 3 or less (1, 2, or 3) and your Style V count is 4 or more (4, 5, or 6). You prefer to perform your responsibilities in a manner that is action oriented and practical. You prefer to work where things happen quickly and results are seen immediately.
- **Yellow.**   Your style color is probably Yellow if your Style H count is 3 or less (1, 2, or 3) and your Style V count is 3 or less (1, 2, or 3). You prefer to perform your responsibilities in a manner that is orderly and planned to meet a known schedule. You prefer to work where things get done with a minimum of interpretations and unexpected change.

Now, place an "S," indicating your style color, in the appropriate quadrant of the Life Style Grid® on the previous page.

Applying Your Symbols

Now that you have a color for retirement interests and a color for style, what do they mean?

Your Interest Color

If your interest color suggests the same activities as the memories exercise, then you will want to pay special attention to exploring the retirement options from this book that are described as consistent with your interest color.

Birkman® organizes the "I" symbol, retirement interests, as shown in the Retirement Interests Grid.

Retirement Interests

Red likes to:	Green likes to:
Build Organize See a finished product Solve a practical problem Work through people	Sell and promote Persuade Motivate people Counsel or teach Work with people
Yellow likes to:	**Blue likes to:**
Schedule activities Do detailed work Keep close control Work with numbers Work with systems	Plan activities Deal with abstraction Think of new approaches Innovate Work with ideas

TM

As you begin to reflect on the activities you are drawn to, you will want to consider whether they contain aspects of the *interests* you are likely to wish to use. If your retirement interest is Green, for example, you will likely feel natural in an environment that calls for persuasion.

Your Style Color

Your style symbol (S) describes how others might describe you. It shows how you like to act, indicating your active behavior. Knowing the style in which you tend to pursue your interests is the first step toward *describing the way in which you would like to pursue your interests.* Your style color adds extra insight for possible retirement activities. It is not uncommon for a person's interest and style colors to be different. A person may like the types of responsibilities associated with their interest but prefer to practice these responsibilities in a manner and within an environment that is consistent with their style. For example, a combination of Green interest and Blue style suggests a retirement that includes persuasive interest performed in a humanistic, creative, and supportive manner. This is a person who likes selling, promoting, persuading, and group-contact responsibilities but who will be most comfortable with a cause or a product in which he holds conviction. A person with a Red interest would likely be drawn to an active retirement, say a visible leadership role on a board. If her style is Blue, however, she will likely need some downtime to withdraw and reflect on the meaning of proposals, while someone with a Red interest–Red style combination might maintain an entirely proactive position. Someone who has a Red interest and a Yellow style may be drawn to a leadership role but is likely to operate conservatively with a close eye on the bottom line.

Birkman® divides the style, or active behavior, as shown in this chart.

Active Behavior

Red appears:	Green appears:
Objective about people Commanding Competitive Practical Forceful	Personable Directive Outspoken Independent Enthusiastic about new things
Yellow appears:	**Blue appears:**
Sociable Orderly Cooperative Consistent Cautious	Perceptive Agreeable Conscientious Reflective Creative

TM

   When we use the Birkman® model in seminars, we separate the colors and then divide a page into two columns as follows. In the left-hand column, we define some characteristics that people associate with a specific color, for example, Red interests, and on the right, we list the tasks and fields of interest that these interests might correspond with.

   Note that these lists were compiled after a brainstorming session at a seminar and demonstrate the way brainstorming works to enlarge concepts. To apply this idea, it is best for you to do your own associations, perhaps by creating a small group of friends or colleagues to work with.

Red Interests	Red Fields
Doing	Working part-time
Building	Serving on Board of Directors
Implementing	Traveling
Organizing	Leading philanthropic efforts
Producing	
Delegating	
Leading	

Green Interests	Green Fields
Motivating	Mentoring
Meditating	Teaching
Selling	Leadership role in spiritual
Influencing	community
Consensus building	
Persuading	
Debating	
Delegating authority	

Yellow Interests	Yellow Fields
Ordering	Working part-time
Numbering	(bookkeeper, local politics)
Scheduling	Volunteering for civic
Systematizing	organization
Preserving	Child caretaker
Maintaining	
Measuring	
Specifying details	

Blue Interests	Blue Fields
Abstracting	Writing a book
Theorizing	Joining spiritual community

Designing   Teaching
Writing   Volunteering
Reflecting
Originating

Similarly, we might list adjectives describing each color style in the left-hand column and translate them on the right.

Red Style   Preferred Environment

Straightforward   Self-structured
Assertive   High pressure
Logical   Hierarchical
Personable   Production oriented
Authoritative   Competitive
Friendly
Direct
Resourceful

Green Style   Preferred Environment

Spontaneous   Team oriented
Talkative   Adventurous
Personal   Informal
Enthusiastic   Innovative
Convincing   Big picture oriented
Risk taking   Varied
Competitive

Yellow Style   Preferred Environment

Cautious   Predictable
Structured   Established
Loyal   Controlled
Systematic   Measurable
Solitary   Orderly
Methodical
Organized

Blue Style	Preferred Environment
Insightful	Cutting edge
Reflective	Informally paced
Selectively sociable	Organized in private offices
Creative	Low key
Thoughtful	Future oriented
Emotional	
Imaginative	
Sensitive	

Characteristics of My Interest Color

Describe my interests.

_____

_____

_____

_____

How would these apply to my day-to-day life postretirement?

_____

_____

_____

_____

What would be my potential activities/interests in retirement?

_____

_____

_____

_____

_____

Characteristics of My Style Group

How do I act, and what style do I exhibit when things are going well?

_____

_____

_____

_____

How would this apply day to day postretirement?

_____

_____

_____

_____

How would this affect my potential activities/interests?

_____

_____

_____

_____

As you isolate your interests and style and reflect on how they may be translated into specific activities and interests in your NewLife, you may want to ask yourself the following questions:

What constructive action should I take?

_____

_____

_____

_____

_____

_____

_____

What strengths would I like to develop, based on my interest and style colors?

_____

_____

_____

_____

_____

_____

_____

How can I seek opportunities to do this?

_____

_____

_____

_____

_____

_____

You are now developing a vocabulary to describe yourself: what interests you and how you have applied these interests as well as what your style is at its best and how you might apply it. As you isolate your major interests and style, what further self-analysis may be required?

Using Your Interest Color and Style Color Estimates

Now that you have an estimate of your interest and style colors, you are ready to use them to begin exploring possible retirement pursuits. As you use your interest and style colors, please remember that they are just estimates; as such, you should not make significant life choices based solely on them. These estimates are to be used as guides to help you explore possibilities. You will want to compare and work in conjunction with the other tools in *Your Retirement, Your Way*, such as your own history, which you analyzed in the previous chapter. As you continue through the book, remembering your interest and style colors will help guide you toward your best and most productive retirement.

Your Memories Revisited

Now think about your memories again. Is there any overlap between your Birkman® profile and the interests and style in your story?

In Paul's Birkman® NewLife style summary, for example, his interests are Green, which signifies that he's a communicator and likes to work with others to get results, and his style is Blue, which shows that he's a planner. In relating his story about fixing his first car, we can see that Paul's Green interests were totally fulfilled; he had promoted a project that grabbed his friend's attention. The project also required concentrated time and energy and creative planning, characteristically appealing to his Blue style. His needs were more subtle. "Partly I was relieved at not failing, not making anything worse. But even more deeply, I enjoyed creating solutions to problems, whether mechanical or human," he said. "The environment was one in which I felt like an explorer and my friend felt like an expert, so that together we had defined exciting roles. Furthermore, we were working on a mechanical project, something with a beginning and an end, yet in an atmosphere in which we could take as long as we needed." Paul's analysis provides important clues about what he needs to feel generally fulfilled.

In comparing Carol's memory to her Birkman® profile, her occupational interests were Green (selling, persuading, promoting), suggesting the promotional elements in the photo she sent to her mother, "so she could enjoy my success." Her style was Red (organizing, producing), suggesting a strong need to convert her experiences into tasks and her desire to manage in such a way that she brings operations to completion. What doesn't show on her Birkman® grid, but emerged through her memory and discussion with her friends, was her need for aesthetic expression. Trained as a technical marketer of home products and highly rewarded and accomplished in that field, she wanted to be more challenged in creative and aesthetic ways in her postwork career. In her NewLife, she has started her own part-time catering business, delivering prepared, healthy dinners to multitasking customers who otherwise don't have time to shop, chop, and cook, a career that she believes wouldn't have occurred to her without doing her "homework."

How does your Birkman® profile coordinate with the interests, style, skills, and needs you've isolated from your story or depository of treasured memories? Take a moment to jot down your thoughts here:

You've done a lot of thinking and writing in this chapter. The sweat equity you put into your retirement development process at this juncture will guide you in subsequent chapters, as you begin to understand your retirement fulfillment profile and use it to set goals and implement your plans for the future.

If you need even more insight, try writing about and dissecting the other "flow" memories you listed previously, according to your needs, interests, style, and skills. What patterns do you see emerging? How do these memories correspond with your Birkman® scores?

Now, take a few minutes to summarize for yourself what you have learned about yourself in the last two chapters. This time, do it in your own words.

Later, you will refer to this summary as you proceed through more of your retirement-planning exercises. These insights will guide you as you begin the strategic-planning process to create your postretirement NewLife.

5

Envisioning Your NewLife

John Trauth

We are confronted with insurmountable opportunities.

—POGO, COMIC STRIP PHILOSOPHER

Documenting Your Dreams

After completing the self-analysis exercises, including the memory and flow analysis and the mini-Birkman®, you now have a clearer idea of your interests, working style, and needs. And chances are that, on your own, you have already given some or even a lot of thought to what you might do after you stop working full-time.

This chapter will help you take your previous thinking and put it together with the new insights you now have and create a "vision" for your NewLife.

The first exercise is very simple. Take a few minutes to write a short vision statement of what you envision your NewLife will be like five years after you officially "retire" from full-time work. Take into account what you have learned about yourself in the last two chapters. Presume that you have made all of the necessary transitions (which we will discuss in Chapter 9, "Planning Your Transition"), everything has worked out just as you planned, your finances are sufficient for your NewLife, and you are living the life of your dreams. Keep the description general, but include the major things you have been dreaming about doing after you retire from full-time work. Try to envision a clear sense of purpose for your NewLife. Dream big and be optimistic. Be passionate. Make it exciting. This is the life you have been waiting for all of your life. Just go for it! And don't worry about the money. We will address that later. Use the space below.

My NewLife Draft Vision Statement

Here is how I will live my NewLife:

Five years after retiring, I will . . . _____

_____

_____

_____

_____

_____

_____

_____

_____

_____

Now, you will begin the process of getting yourself from here to there.

Charting Your OldLife

The first thing to do is to chart your OldLife. There are 168 hours in a week (7 days × 24 hours). Fifty-six of those, more or less, you are asleep, and let's say that another twelve of those are spent in transitional activities. That leaves 100 hours to allocate, which does not count your time off for vacations (you will add this time back into the allocation later). One hundred hours is probably unrealistic, because there are always distractions and inefficiencies, but 100 is a nice round number, so we'll use it for the purpose of this exercise.

Please refer to Figure 5.1 and allocate those 100 hours by percentages into the categories shown. Remember that the percentages will need to add up to 100. Use a pencil so that you can make changes later.

1. **Work and Income-Producing Activities.**   This is the amount of time you spend earning income. For example, if you are working 40 hours a week, then your time allocation to this category would be 40 percent.
2. **Family.**   This is the percentage of the week you spend with your family and doing family activities during the week, not counting time alone with your spouse/significant other. How many hours a day are you together? Make sure to include time on weekends. If your children no longer live with you, and you don't see them regularly except for vacations, then this time might only cover phone calls. We will add "visits with family" back in later during vacation time. Other family activities include housework, yard work, and balancing your checkbook.

Figure 5.1   *OldLife and NewLife Chart*

Category	Percentage Before	Goals	Percentage After
Work	☐	_____ _____ _____	☐
Family	☐	_____ _____ _____	☐
Couple	☐	_____ _____ _____	☐
Friends	☐	_____ _____ _____	☐
Community	☐	_____ _____ _____	☐
Personal	☐	_____ _____ _____	☐
Totals	**100%**	_____	**100%**

3. **Couple.** This category is for you and your spouse or life partner. How much time are you together in a week? It doesn't have to be "quality time." It doesn't matter if this is just watching TV together. Again, remember to add in the weekend time. (Note: If you live alone, this category is either zero or whatever time you spend trying to find a significant other, in which case, you could label this category "romance." Otherwise, this time belongs in the "personal" category.)

4. **Friends.** Time with friends can include meeting at the gym after work or going out for lunch or dinner or weekend activities. Do not include professional acquaintances in this category, unless your professional and personal friendships truly overlap.

5. **Community.** This category includes the average number of hours per week that you spend on community issues. This can include your time on nonprofit boards, religious activities, volunteering for favorite causes, going to city council meetings, coaching at your local high school, anything that involves participation in community activities. Your definition of "community" can be as big or as small as you want it to be (from national political activity to local causes, from nonprofit board leadership to individual mentoring, and everything in between.)

6. **Personal.** This is time just for you. It could include athletics, reading, learning new things like playing an instrument, and personal travel. It also includes unstructured downtime.

Using Figure 5.1, "OldLife and NewLife Chart," allocate your 100 hours of your OldLife to these six categories under the "Percentage Before" column. Again, remember that the percentages need to add up to 100 percent.

Now, think for a moment about the time you spend during vacations and holidays. For ease of calculation, use ten holidays a year (100 hours) and whatever number of weeks of true vacation that you plan to take (100 hours times × number of weeks). No, all of your retirement is not "vacation." This is the time when you get away from your normal routine and do things like travel, spend time at your vacation home, or go on a hiking and camping expedition. Because there are fifty-two weeks in a year and you are allocating a total of 5,200 hours, calculate the approximate percentage of time that vacations and holidays, however you spend them, would change your previous allocations if they were added to a typical week. You can even use 5,000 hours if that makes the mental calculations easier. You don't need a high level of accuracy here; you just need approximations.

For example, if "couple" time is currently 10 percent of your weekly routine, and you also spend an additional 200 hours with your life partner during holidays and vacations, divide 200 by 5,000, which equals 4 percent. Then add that 4 percent to your previous 10 percent to come up with 14 percent for couple time. Of course, you will have to subtract 4 percent from other categories to ensure that the total still adds up to 100 percent.

Note: Another way of doing this entire exercise would be to start with 5,200 hours and allocate against that number, but we think it is easier to do the weekly analysis and then adjust it later.

You have now made your estimates and your refinements. Take a look at your OldLife Chart. Reflect on it for a few minutes. Now fill in the following chart, specifying what you like about your OldLife and what you don't like.

I Like	*I Don't Like*
1.	1.
2.	2.
3.	3.
4.	4.
5.	5.
6.	6.
7.	7.
8.	8.

Charting Your NewLife

Now comes the fun part. At some specific point, most likely when you decide to stop working full-time, you will have the opportunity to reallocate these categories according to your wishes.

Perhaps you want to take some true vacation time after you officially retire. This is a great idea. Don't overanalyze it, just *do it!* Take whatever time you want. Enjoy it. Travel. Play golf or tennis or squash. Ski. Go to the beach. Or just relax. You've earned it.

Realistically, however, you can't do this forever. While it may look like the ideal life, it isn't. Just ask anyone who has done it. At some point, you need to come back to the real world, reconnect, and continue to be productive, contribute, learn, and grow. As we mentioned earlier, studies have shown that extending your productive life is likely to result in both a happier and a longer life. The alternatives are not very attractive.

So let's presume you have taken some time off, and it was great. Now you are back, and it's time to get back in the action . . . but this time, it's on your terms!

Let's begin with the same categories that you just analyzed for your OldLife. First, you need to establish "goals" for each of these categories. Then you will reallocate your time to accomplish these goals.

To help you get started, here is a brief primer on goals, strategies, objectives, and activities:

- **Goals** are the *overall results* you want to achieve, like "Bond with my grandchild." You could think of each goal as a personal destination.
- **Strategies** are the directions and methodology you plan to use to move toward your goals. A properly constructed set of strategies will keep you focused. Some people refer to these as "core strategies." For example, one of your strategies for bonding with your grandchild might be "Find occasions to talk about the important lessons I learned while growing up," or "Find ways to support his or her interest in swimming." A good set of strategies will start you in the right direction and, one hopes, keep you going in that direction. Strategies should also not be in conflict with your goals. A strategy of "Live abroad for a year" is probably in conflict with your goal to bond with your grandchild, unless you take him or her with you!

- **Objectives** are like subgoals with *measurable* outcomes that usually—though not always—will get you to your goals. For example, one objective for the goal of bonding with your grandchild might be "Spend six weekends hiking with my grandchild next year." At the end of the year, or whatever specific time period you have chosen, you can count your weekend hiking trips together and see whether you achieved your objective. On the other hand, if you discover that your grandchild does not enjoy overnight camping, you might want to consider modifying the objective either to day hikes or to another measurable outcome that is more likely to achieve your overall goal. If he or she loves to swim, your new objective might be six weekends together at the beach or pool.
- **Activities and Tasks** are the specific actions you plan to take in pursuit of your goals, consistent with your strategies and objectives. Examples might be "Buy my grandchild private swimming lessons," "Attend swimming practices and swim meets," or "Take him or her to the beach on Saturdays." Many different activities can help you achieve your objectives and realize your goals.

We'll come back to strategies, objectives, and activities in Chapter 7, "Constructing Your NewLife Road Map." In Chapter 11, "Evaluating Your NewLife Progress and Making Course Corrections," we give you a system for evaluating your progress toward your goals and making sure that your strategies, objectives, and tasks/activities are really helping you to get to your desired destination.

For right now, set your personal goals in each of the following categories. Don't begin the reallocation of time yet;

just finish writing down goals for each of the categories in Figure 5.1, your OldLife and NewLife Chart.

1. **Work and Income-Producing Activities.**   You spent an enormous part of your life preparing for your career. This is one of the ways you have made a contribution to society. How can you apply what you have learned to your NewLife? It is time to write down your goals for your new professional life. How can you continue to stay involved? Perhaps you can consult with your old company. Perhaps you would rather start a new, part-time career in the same industry, but with another bigger (or smaller) company. Perhaps you want to start your own company and/or consulting practice. Perhaps you want to work less but raise your hourly rates. Perhaps you want to take your skills and apply them in a different industry. Or perhaps you have created a product that you can continue to promote on a commission basis. (Note: If your plan is to contribute your expertise for free, then this goal belongs in the "community" category.) If you plan to stop working entirely, then this is your goal.

2. **Family.**   What are your goals for your family? Do you want to re-bond with your kids or spend more time with grandchildren? Do you have relatives you would like to spend more time with? Do you want or need to mentor someone in your family in some fashion, either in a positive sense (helping achieve potential) or a negative sense (helping fight an addiction)?

3. **Couple.**   Now is your chance to spend more time together and deepen your relationship with your life partner. What will you do? What common interests can you pursue with more intensity than before? As you

think about this, remember the adage, "For better or worse, but not for lunch." In other words, each person needs personal space. Don't make a plan that suffocates either of you. We'll discuss this more in the next chapter, "Sharing and Validating Your Dreams."

4. **Friends.**   Here is the opportunity to build on your existing friendships as well as make new ones. Friendships are one of the most essential building blocks of a happy life. Remember that your friends may not have the same amount of time as you do, and some friendships are stronger when they are occasional, related to a specific subject or occasion, and not time intensive. So think carefully about your goals for this category.

5. **Community.**   Do you want to "give back" to your community? If so, what do you want to do to make a difference? These opportunities may not appear all at once, and, if they do, you will need to spend some time sorting out what you want to do (and not do). Define this category broadly. Opportunities could include becoming more involved with your coop or homeowners association; participating in volunteer work; being on nonprofit boards; volunteering for activities with your church, synagogue, or mosque; or making another type of contribution to your community, however you define it.

6. **Personal.**   What are your personal goals for your NewLife? Have you always wanted to do or learn something that you never had time for? Play a new sport? Learn a foreign language? Play a musical instrument? Add in the new, but don't forget the old. What did you do in this category in the past? For example, if staying in shape was one of your prime activities, chances are that you will want to continue that activity. But remem-

ber that adding in new ones will obviously increase the time in this category.

Once you have completed writing down all of your goals for each of the six categories, read them again and make sure they are really *goals* and not strategies, objectives, or activities. These are the overall results you want to achieve, the destination you want to attain, the *big* picture—*not* the methodology or actions to get you there.

Once you are comfortable with your goals, go back to Figure 5.1 and reallocate the percentage of time you estimate you will be spending in each category to achieve your goals. While you are doing this, also review the list you made about what you like and don't like about your OldLife. The idea here is to maximize happiness in your NewLife by adding things you like and getting rid of the things you don't like.

Your total time allocation is still limited to 100 percent. If you add time to one category, it has to come out of the others somewhere. But don't worry—we are all living longer these days, so think of your goals as multiyear goals (further discussed below).

For example, my OldLife and NewLife Chart is shown in Figure 5.2. Note that, in my chart, the allocations for family and personal did not change from OldLife to NewLife. It was working, and I didn't want to change it. If it ain't broke, don't fix it!

Now, look at your NewLife goals and allocations. Do they seem overly optimistic? Good. They should. Don't worry about that for now. We will do the reality check in Chapter 7, "Constructing Your NewLife Road Map." For the moment, just let yourself be excited by all of the things you might do and become. It is a little like starting your life over again. As Dr. Seuss said, "Oh! The places you'll go!"

So for now, paraphrasing Pogo, just let yourself be confronted with all of the wonderful "insurmountable opportunities!"

Figure 5.2   **John's OldLife and NewLife Chart**

Category	Percentage Before	Goals	Percentage After
Work	50%	Work half-time	25%
		Take on only interesting work	
Family	10%	Stay close to New York family	10%
		Deepen bond with Eric & Carrie	
Couple	15%	Maintain strong marriage	25%
		Help Astrid maintain good health	
		Travel together 8 weeks/year	
Friends	5%	Deepen friendship with Dave, Jan	10%
		Maintain friendship with Alan	
		Renew 1 old friendship each year	
Community	5%	Serve as president,	15%
		QC Foundation	
		Serve on 3 to 4 other non-	
		profit boards	
Personal	15%	Stay in shape	15%
		Take a personal day each month	
Totals	**100%**		**100%**

Updating Your Vision Statement

The last exercise in this chapter is to update the original vision statement you wrote for yourself. Now that you have analyzed your time allocations in your OldLife, written your specific NewLife goals in each of the six categories, and made your initial reallocations of time, go back and reread the vision statement you wrote at the beginning of this chapter. With your NewLife goals in mind, and remembering your Birkman® results and your insights from the memories exercises, rewrite your vision statement below. Remember, this is the overall statement of your dream life in retirement. But first, I'll give you mine as an example.

John's NewLife Vision Statement

Here is how I will live my NewLife:

Five years after retiring, I will be working no more than half-time, averaging twenty hours a week, taking on only meaningful work that I enjoy and that contributes to society. I will visit my family in New York and Los Angeles frequently. I will maintain my strong marriage, spending more time with my wife, including a month a year in Paris. I will be actively involved in meaningful causes in San Francisco. I will be active athletically and in good shape. I will maintain five close friendships. I will maintain my fluency in French. I will love my life and look forward to every new day with passion and excitement.

Now it's your turn. Write your NewLife vision statement in the space provided.

NewLife Vision Statement

Here is how I will live my NewLife:

Five years after retiring, I will . . . _____

_____

_____

_____

_____

_____

_____

_____

_____

_____

_____

_____

If you have done your job well, your vision statement should excite you. After you have had time to internalize it, you may feel that it has a sense of its own gravity, that it is pulling you toward it. This is what you want to be and to become.

The next step is to start sharing and validating your dream life.

6

Sharing and Validating Your Dreams

Alan Bernstein

If you want to lift yourself up, lift someone else up.

—BOOKER T. WASHINGTON,
TEACHER, AUTHOR

As we've discussed in previous chapters, the decision to retire is one of the most significant choices you will make during the course of your lifetime. As with most decisions you have made, however, this is a step you cannot take alone. Looking back over your life, your goals and dreams could not have been achieved without the support of family, advisers, teachers, and colleagues. Some people had more influence than others, while others had wiser counsel. And occasionally, it took some strategic cajoling to convince a loved one that, yes, you really were leaving the accounting firm to pursue your dream of starting an avocado farm.

What is your dream today? Retirement is not static. It is a time of unprecedented freedom and flexibility. Your life will evolve away from a work-centered existence toward other worthy pursuits. If 75 percent of your preretirement energy was spent working but only 25 percent will be postretirement, how will you fill that extra time? Where will you direct that energy now? Today, the opportunities are endless; the choices are so vast that, without a clear strategy and direction, moving forward can become overwhelming.

To make this transition as smooth as possible, the relationships that have defined your life up to this point must open up to support your new endeavors. The set patterns with which you communicate to your boss, your spouse, your immediate family, and the outside community will inevitably need to be adjusted. The dynamic you create with each shifting relationship will in large part determine the ease of reallocating your energies to new pursuits. Is your spouse on board? Do you have the thumbs-up from your boss and colleagues? These relationships must be managed in such a way that you can pursue the opportunities ahead with vigor, confidence, and the emotional support you require.

Converting Your Skills

The Common Retiree Activities worksheet shows a selection of common activities of today's retirees. This is by no means a comprehensive list, but it will get you started in thinking about your options and the people who can help you get there. Write in the names of each person in your life who you need on board to help you accomplish the activities that interest you.

Common Retiree Activities

Teach a class at my local college or community center

Spouse/partner _____

Family member _____

Boss/colleague/friend _____

Member of community* _____

Volunteer at the Boys and Girls Club, YMCA, or similar organization

Spouse/partner _____

Family member _____

Boss/colleague/friend _____

Member of community* _____

Travel locally or to exotic locales

Spouse/partner _____

Family member _____

Boss/colleague/friend _____

Member of community* _____

Work part-time, join the board, or become a mentor in my former career

Spouse/partner _____

Family member _____

Boss/colleague/friend _____

Member of community* _____

Help beautify public gardens and parks

Spouse/partner _____

Family member _____

Boss/colleague/friend _____

Member of community* _____

Take classes or earn a degree in a new field of interest

Spouse/partner _____

Family member _____

Boss/colleague/friend _____

Member of community* _____

Become an occasional caretaker for my grandchildren

Spouse/partner _____

Family member _____

Boss/colleague/friend _____

Member of community* _____

Work part-time or full-time

Spouse/partner _____

Family member _____

Boss/colleague/friend _____

Member of community* _____

Grow spiritually through prayer, study and/or involvement in my local religious community

Spouse/partner _____

Family member _____

Boss/colleague/friend _____

Member of community* _____

Other activity: _____

Spouse/partner _____

Family member _____

Boss/colleague/friend _____

Member of community* _____

_____

*A member of community can be anyone in your life who plays a role outside of the home and work, such as a spiritual leader, yoga instructor, or volunteer leader.

Many of these pursuits involve giving up the traditional role of the worker to give something back. Given your extensive life experience, you are now part of the most skilled generation and have much to offer to those who are younger than you. In fact, postretirement, many retirees choose to continue working part-time or full-time: 37 percent of men and 31 percent of women, according to a recent American Association of Retired Persons (AARP) survey. This may sound counterintuitive—don't retirees usually leave the workforce? But getting a new job postretirement (as opposed to continuing the old job at a reduced level) is much different than continuing a career. It can be just as fulfilling as well as financially rewarding (see Chapter 8). But working postretirement is commonly less time consuming, stressful, and promotion-driven than the career you've built over the course of your lifetime. You might find that you enjoy it now more than before.

Getting Buy-In from Key People

Whatever your goals and dreams may be after retirement, the primary person you probably need to support you through the transition is your spouse or life partner. Retirement can be a difficult challenge for many relationships. How will the roles you have spent many years playing differ once one or both of you are at home? Do you retire simultaneously, or does one of you continue working? How much time do you spend together now that you are free of the daily obligation of going to the office? What happens if one spouse wants to travel the world while the other wants to stay close to home and spend more time with family?

The key to maintaining a solid, supportive relationship during this crucial change is obvious: communication. This may sound simplistic. After all, what is marriage but a relationship of constant communication and compromise? This may be true in most cases, but the profound transition of one or both spouses retiring is, like having children, a change that alters not only your role in the relationship but also your identity. In fact, the challenge has proved so great that, according to the *Wall Street Journal*, the divorce rate for married couples over fifty-five is now higher than that of the rest of the population (February 2005).

The decision to retire may have been an internal conversation up until this point. Perhaps you and your spouse have discussed it in passing. Now is the time to sit down without any distractions and discuss all of the foreseeable challenges you face if one or both of you retires. By evoking a communication style of consultation with your partner, he or she is much more likely to be open and supportive. And your success and happiness in retirement will be that much more assured.

Ruth and Dan's story illustrates the dangers of not communicating how you envision your retirement.

> Ruth and Dan had both looked forward to Dan's upcoming retirement from the bank. A stay-at-home mom for so many years, Ruth especially had anticipated spending this long-awaited time focusing on their marriage after so many years of struggling to get their kids off into the world. She envisioned evenings talking by the fire, planning the trips they would take and making plans for the future. Dan, although he assumed he and Ruth would spend more time together in some capacity, longed for sunny days on the golf course and starting that deck he had been planning to build.
>
> However, the reality of Dan's retirement was vastly different than they had individually envisioned. After virtually a lifetime of going into the office each day, Dan did not have a plan for allocating his day-to-day activities. He golfed a good amount, of course, but more often he was home alone. Ruth, for her part, did not understand, as she

called it, "his obsession with golfing." Resenting his time on the course, she spent most of her days doing what she had always done when he was at work: having lunch with friends, shopping, and planning her garden. They were only really together in the evenings, but the air was now thick with their mutual resentment.

"Why doesn't he spend more time with me now that he has the time to spend? Obviously, he'd rather be golfing," Ruth said to herself.

"Every time I come home, she's off with her friends. It obviously doesn't matter to her that I've gone and retired," Dan fumed.

After about a month had passed, these thoughts became words. The ensuing argument was ugly, but once their anger passed, they found that they had each misinterpreted the other's actions. As time passed, each put out small efforts that eventually brought them closer. Ruth learned to golf, and, although she knew she would never love it, she looked at it as going on long walks with her husband. Dan would occasionally join his wife on her jaunts around town. More importantly, by finally communicating, they learned how to spend time apart without resentment and to enjoy their time together all the more.

What could Dan and Ruth have done differently to avoid their postretirement period of anger and resentment? Before facing retirement, each spouse had very specific roles to play in the marriage. Their daily lives were, for the most part, lived separately. Dan did not consult Ruth on his business affairs, just as Ruth did not answer to Dan about what to cook for dinner and how to dress the kids. The separate spheres kept the peace, but they did not prepare the couple for the consultative nature of retirement.

Think about the big changes and events, such as having children, changing jobs, and relocating, that you and your partner have gone through over the years. By now your style of communication has probably solidified into a well-defined pattern. This pattern may work for everyday decisions, but discussing a change as complex as planning for the rest of your lives will take special care and thought. In any intense discussion where the stakes are high, it can be difficult to prevent emotions from taking over, foiling constructive communication. In the following exercise, check off whether you or your spouse (or both) is more likely to:

My Communication Style

	Me	My Spouse/Partner
Initiate difficult conversations	____	____
Compromise	____	____
Remain rational	____	____
Give in to avoid a fight	____	____
Become angry	____	____
Concede	____	____
Bring up past grudges	____	____
Consult outside parties	____	____
Become tearful	____	____
Make a joke/add humor	____	____
Clam up/walk away before resolution	____	____

In discussing your retirement, do you need to change anything about the way you communicate to make this transition as smooth as possible? Is there anything you wish your spouse would change in this regard? Remember that the goal is to create a collaborative environment in which you can feel confident about taking this next step together.

Negotiating this, or any change, is a skill like any other: the more you prepare, the better you'll become. Actively think about how you and your life partner communicate the next time you go to the movies or make a decision about an upcoming vacation. Note how, even in a seemingly inconsequential discussion, each party can choose to be "conversationally generous" or "conversationally neglectful." Tone, body language, and timing all play a key role in how a discussion plays itself out.

- Does each of you give your full listening attention to the other?
- Do you maintain eye contact when the other is speaking?
- Is either of you overly dismissive to the other's ideas?
- Do either of you tend to interrupt the other or talk over the other?
- When your spouse is speaking, do you think about what you are going to say next instead of really listening?
- Do you employ touch when in a heated discussion, such as a conciliatory touch of the hand?
- Do you gracefully accept the other's weaknesses, or is either of you accusatory?
- Are you both willing to compromise, or does someone have to "win"?

You can make a copy of this list of questions and have it close at hand. Give one to your spouse so that you can both work on creating an emotionally safe environment in which to plan your future.

Coordinating Different Visions

It's a long shot that your vision of the retirement years ahead will perfectly match what your loved ones are visualizing. Thus, the need for clear and supportive communication is imperative. But prioritizing your goals is crucial in creating the compromises that will ensure a satisfying retirement (not to mention a happy marriage and family life).

For example, it may be absolutely imperative for you to live the six months of winter in Florida. It also could be important that you golf every weekend, excluding holidays. And it's possible that you prefer to babysit the grandkids no more than once a month. If your wife wants to move next door to the grandkids in Ohio to help out every afternoon, how are you going to compromise? What is really and truly important to you? Choosing your battles wisely is, as you likely know, the key to maintaining a peaceful marriage. Prioritizing your retirement goals is another way of expressing that very same sentiment.

Getting to Agreement

The following priority analysis exercise originated in *What Color Is Your Parachute?* by Richard Bolles. This exercise will help you prioritize your goals, and it can become a negotiating tool with your spouse or partner. Refer back to the goals you set for yourself in Chapter 5 on your NewLife Chart. Make a list of the six goals that are most important for you to achieve a fulfilling retirement. List them here in any order.

My Goals (not in order)

1. _____

2. _____

3. _____

4. _____

5. _____

6. _____

In the following grid, each number corresponds to an item you listed. Within each box, circle the number that represents your preferred retirement goal. For example, if (1) is "work 20 hours a week" and (2) is "travel 6 months a year" becoming a board member at your old company, you have to decide which is more important to you in that top box.

1 2				
1 3	2 3			
1 4	2 4	3 4		
1 5	2 5	3 5	4 5	
1 6	2 6	3 6	4 6	5 6

How many circles did each item receive? The more times you circled an item, the higher a priority it is to you. Now, list your retirement goals according to the priority level of each one.

My Goals (in priority order)

1. _____
2. _____
3. _____
4. _____
5. _____
6. _____

Again, this exercise is a tool that should help you clearly prioritize your retirement goals. What is most important? What is negotiable? What can you absolutely not live without? If these distinctions are clear in your mind, any discussion you have with your spouse is more likely to be direct and constructive. You can state your desires with confidence and know where to bend to your partner's set of priorities.

Your negotiation skills will not only come in handy with your spouse, however. The decision to retire will profoundly affect your immediate family as well. If your priorities are unclear and your communication skills inadequate, it is inevitable that conflicts will arise. A good example is the case of Sandra and Beth.

Beth and her mother, Sandra, both lived in the same small town in Minnesota. Married with three small children,

Beth was thrilled to learn that Sandra was retiring within the year. She had her regular babysitters, but what could be better (and cheaper!) than having the kids' grandmother to rely on?

Sandra was sincerely looking forward to spending more time with her daughter and grandkids. What grandmother wouldn't? She also was planning to join various organizations within her community with her friend Gladys and wanted to get her tennis game in shape, not to mention her garden and the trip to Belize with her boyfriend. Sandra was ambitious about all she wanted to do now that she was free of full-time employment. She was also one of those people who can't say no.

Beth never thought twice about leaving the kids with her mom when she wanted to go to the store or when she needed to take the dog to the vet. And she and her husband needed their date night, right? Sandra ended up scratching her trip to Belize and was too ashamed to return Gladys' calls asking why she had missed meetings. She did not plan on becoming a full-time babysitter for the kids. But how, as a loving grandmother, could she admit to not wanting to be so involved? How could she tell Beth to not always assume that she was available? She was equally as offended by her daughter's presumption as she was ashamed by her own—as she perceived it—selfishness.

After reading this chapter, you can probably guess how Sandra could have avoided the situation in which she found herself. Her daughter is not her direct partner with whom she was planning out her retirement. However, she is an important individual in Sandra's life and Sandra needed her buy-in for her retirement plan. Had Sandra sat down with Beth and communicated her retirement priorities, Beth would have understood that there were limits to Sandra's willingness to babysit. Many hurt feelings and misunderstandings would have been prevented.

Imagine that we are looking at Sandra's list of her six retirement goals, and bonding with the grandkids was the number-three goal on her list, after community service and travel. All of these goals are extremely broad, however, as your list probably is, because goals are supposed to be broad. If Sandra had broken down goal number three to make it more specific and had included her intended strategies and activities, she may have had an even better understanding of what she needed to express to Beth.

Sandra's Goals:
3. Spending time with Jill, Billy, and Kate

Strategies/Activities:
(a) Care for them one afternoon or evening per week
(b) Make special efforts to expose them to cultural activities
(c) Start teaching them French

From this example, Sandra's vision of caring for her grandchildren becomes much more specific.

In the following exercise, break down each of your six prioritized retirement goals into subcategories, including strategies and activities. Provide as many details as possible to give life and depth to what you envision.

My Goals (in priority order, with details)

1. _____

    (a) _____

    (b) _____

    (c) _____

2. _____

    (a) _____

    (b) _____

    (c) _____

3. _____

    (a) _____

    (b) _____

    (c) _____

4. _____

    (a) _____

    (b) _____

    (c) _____

5. _____

    (a) _____

    (b) _____

    (c) _____

6. _____

    (a) _____

    (b) _____

    (c) _____

Remember that the detail with which you describe your goals, whether you are discussing them with your spouse, colleague, son, or daughter, will make your wishes clearer and potentially more convincing and attainable.

This chapter has started you on the path to answering two of the most crucial retirement questions: what are my priority goals and who will help me attain them? You now know what is important to you and how you can respectfully and successfully get those you love on board for the journey. Such preparation is crucial to entering into this dynamic stage of life and has laid the groundwork for the coming chapters. You have the "what" and the "who." All you need now is the "how," which you will begin to learn in Chapter 7.

Constructing Your NewLife Road Map

John Trauth

Vision without action is hallucination.

—Attribution unknown

By now you should be feeling that you have a much better idea of what you want your NewLife to be like and how you would like to spend your time to achieve your NewLife goals. If you have followed the prescriptions in the previous chapter, you have taken steps to insure that the important people in your life are supportive of the conceptual NewLife you have created for yourself. The next step is to develop the road map, which is the plan that will get you there.

The Long and the Short of It All

Because a goal is a general statement of what you want to accomplish, it is generally associated with a longer-time perspective. For example, "Learn to speak French fluently" is not a goal that you are likely to accomplish in the first year of retirement, unless you move to a French-speaking country and immerse yourself in the language and culture—a strategy that probably is in conflict with some of your other goals. To make your plan real, you need to add both "actions" and "time horizons" that will provide you with a meaningful plan of action as well as the ability to measure your progress.

The actions are the strategies and tasks/activities, and the time horizons are the objectives. As I mentioned in Chapter 1, Dave Corbett, who runs New Directions, a company that helps people with life transitions, calls these objectives "dreams with deadlines."

Now it's time to add some strategies, activities, and deadlines to your dreams. For each of your goals, you will develop both strategies and objectives, first in a five-year horizon and then for the first year.

Go back now and reread the vision statement that you wrote at the end of Chapter 5. Remember that this is how you envisioned your ideal NewLife five years after retiring.

Now, refer back to the goals you prioritized in Chapter 6, and write them in the left-hand column of Figure 7.1.

Next, for each goal, describe your "core strategies," which are the essential actions that you plan to take to achieve your five-year goals. Refer again back to your work in Chapter 6. List them in the second column. Do this for all of your priority goals. To help you decide what actions you want to take, reread the description of strategies in Chapter 5, in the "Documenting Your Dreams" section.

In the third column, write down your five-year objectives. Remember that these must be measurable accomplishments.

You must also feel that you have a realistic possibility of accomplishing these objectives in five years. For relationship goals, like "bonding with my grandchild," the objectives may be less quantitatively measurable than for your other goals, but describe the characteristics and/or the quality of the relationship you want to create through your core strategies.

After you have finished, take a fresh look at what you have written and ask yourself the following questions:

- Are any of my goals in conflict with each other? If so, how can I resolve these conflicts, given my priorities?
- Will my strategies really help me reach my goals?
- Are all of my objectives measurable?
- Am I being too aggressive and trying to do too much? If so, what should I either eliminate or postpone?

After you have made any adjustments, you have the first conceptual draft of your five-year road map. But don't panic—it is not set in stone. You will have a number of opportunities to go back and revise it as we go along.

Creating Your One-Year Plan

Next, we are going to take this down to the one-year level. You need a five-year plan to move you toward your five-year vision. But what are you going to do immediately (or immediately after you retire) to start your journey? This is where the rubber meets the road.

Copy your goals from the left-hand column of Figure 7.1 to the left-hand column of Figure 7.2. Because goals are your

Figure 7.1   *NewLife Five-Year Action Plan*

Five-Year Goals	Core Strategies	Five-Year Objectives
1.	1. _____	1. _____
	2. _____	2. _____
	3. _____	3. _____
2.	1. _____	1. _____
	2. _____	2. _____
	3. _____	3. _____
3.	1. _____	1. _____
	2. _____	2. _____
	3. _____	3. _____
4.	1. _____	1. _____
	2. _____	2. _____
	3. _____	3. _____
5.	1. _____	1. _____
	2. _____	2. _____
	3. _____	3. _____
6.	1. _____	1. _____
	2. _____	2. _____
	3. _____	3. _____

Figure 7.2   **NewLife One-Year Action Plan**

Goals	First-Year Strategies	First-Year Objectives
1.	1.	1.
	2.	2.
	3.	3.
2.	1.	1.
	2.	2.
	3.	3.
3.	1.	1.
	2.	2.
	3.	3.
4.	1.	1.
	2.	2.
	3.	3.
5.	1.	1.
	2.	2.
	3.	3.
6.	1.	1.
	2.	2.
	3.	3.

ultimate destinations, they are the same for your one-year plan as for the five-year plan.

Let's move on to the strategies and objectives. Some people will find it easier to formulate the measurable first-year objectives and then determine what actions (strategies and activities) will be necessary to accomplish their goals. Others will find it easier to think about the actions (strategies and activities) first. (At the one-year level, strategies and activities are similar, so we use both terms here.) It doesn't matter which way you choose to proceed. What does matter is that you make sure that you have only actions you plan to take in the first year as strategies/activities and only measurable accomplishments as first-year objectives. Using Figure 7.2, write down your one-year strategies and objectives.

For example, Ken has a goal to get in better shape. To achieve this goal, here is how he might put together his strategies and objectives.

First-Year Goals	Strategies	First-Year Objectives
1. Get in better shape	1. Join a gym	1. Lose 15 pounds
	2. Employ a personal trainer	2. Bench press my body weight
	3. Join a running club	3. Run and finish two 10k races

Let's look at another, somewhat more intangible example. One of Chris's goals is to get more involved in her community, but she is not sure exactly how to go about it. In this case, Chris's strategies and objectives are more process driven.

Goal	First-Year Strategies	First-Year Objective
1. Become more involved in my community	1. Collect a list of local nonprofits 2. Select three of interest 3. Interview the executive directors and other board members 4. Determine where there is mutual interest 5. If necessary, expand list and repeat process	1. Become a board member of a local nonprofit

After you have finished writing your strategies and objectives, take a fresh look at what you have written and ask yourself the following questions:

- Are any of my goals in conflict with each other? If so, how can I resolve these conflicts, given my priorities?
- Will my strategies really help me reach my goals?
- Are all of my objectives measurable?
- Am I being too aggressive and trying to do too much in the first year? If so, what should I either eliminate or postpone?
- To accomplish my first-year objectives, should I go back to my NewLife portion of my OldLife and NewLife Chart and change my time allocations?

It is time to look at each of your goals and develop the details of how you plan to achieve them. Much of this information can be drawn from what you have previously done, but it will help you to focus on each goal individually and to add in not only your strategies but also your activities and tasks. For example, here are the details of Ken's goal about getting in better shape:

Goal: Get in Better Shape

First-Year Objectives	Completion Dates
1. Lose 15 pounds	1. December 24 (this year)
2. Bench press my body weight	2. September 30 (this year)
3. Run and finish two 10k races	3. October 31 (this year)

Strategy	Tasks and Timing	Suggested Activity
Join a gym	Check out Gold's Gym, The Bay Club, and 24-Hour Nautilus. Join one by January 31st.	
Employ a personal trainer	Interview personal trainers in all gyms. Make selection of gym based on this information.	
Join a running club	Identify potential running clubs; join one. Find a running partner to prepare for two local 10k weekend races.	Look in local newspapers and on the Internet for clubs and potential running partners.

Ken now has a very specific, carefully thought-out plan to achieve his goal of getting in better shape. Now do the same thing for each of your goals. Use a separate piece of paper for each goal, using the same format.

Reviewing Your Plans

When you are done, you will have your five-year and one-year plans and the details associated with your strategies and activities for each of your goals. All of the various building blocks from the earlier exercises should feel solidly in place and everything should feel consistent and positive. You may feel some creative tension; that is fine because this is very important, life-changing material. But if you are feeling that something is wrong and your plan isn't all adding up to a life you will enjoy, stop now and go back. The purpose of the retirement master planning process is to help you create a life that you will enjoy and that will make you feel happy and fulfilled.

Review your memories exercises and your Birkman® results again. Are you creating for yourself a life that is consistent with your interests, style, and needs? If you don't feel that you are, then what are the hot spots that make you feel uncomfortable? Are you doing some things because you think that you should or have to, not because you want to? Sometimes this is inevitable (like caring for an aging parent) but other times, and frequently in retirement, it is no longer necessary to live up to the expectations of others. In the latter case, you can make the decision to stop doing the things that don't give you pleasure, even if you are good at those things.

Here is a technique that allows people the freedom to try on different roles and personalities and see how they fit. At the beginning of the experience (like a week-long Outward Bound excursion, for example), participants are asked who knows each other. Then they are separated into different groups so that everyone is new to everyone else. The instructor/facilitator tells the members of each group that, for the next week or other time frame of the experience, they can be whoever they want to be. They can call themselves by a different name. They can take on entirely different personalities. They can act differently. They can experiment with being a different person or act out different aspects of their personality. Because no one else in the group knows what they are "really" like or has any history with them, no one will be prejudging them. Participants can be any way they choose to be for this short time. What inevitably happens is that people find out that they really are who they are, that they can't really change overnight, but that they do have the opportunity to grow in that persona. The freedom to do this is inspiring, and many people leave the experience with new energy to change and improve their lives.

Think of approaching retirement this way. I hope that the exercises have helped you to better understand your personality and what makes you happy. Yes, you can wipe the slate clean and start over, but you are who you are. Use that knowledge to construct a NewLife for yourself that provides the maximum opportunity to make you happy, of which personal growth is a big part. We will discuss that in more depth in the last chapter.

Getting Buy-In for Your Plans

When you are comfortable with your five-year and one-year plans, it is time again to get the important people in your life on board with your plans. If you followed the advice in Chapter 6, you have already gotten buy-in for your NewLife vision from your spouse or life partner, family, friends, and colleagues who will be important to you in the journey ahead.

It may seem obvious, but remember that it is more important to get buy-in from those who will be most closely sharing your journey. Pay particular attention to your life partner and those others who will be most involved.

Your five-year and one-year plans are more specific than your vision statement, so it is more important to review these plans with those closest to you who will be involved on a day-to-day basis. This can help you solidify their support as they begin to understand the specifics of what you are proposing. Sharing your plans with them can also uncover any inconsistencies of perception or potential conflicts that exist between you about what you are planning to do. They may also question your assumptions about whether your strategies will get you to your goals and, if so, in what time frame. They may also suggest ways in which they can be helpful or supportive that you didn't consider. By sharing your plans at this early stage, you make those closest to you part of your plans and create another opportunity to bring them on board and get their support as well as to solicit their active involvement in helping you achieve your NewLife vision.

As your plans take shape, you will find it becoming easier to envision your NewLife lifestyle in more detail. To make it even more real, Chapter 8 will show you how to reorganize your finances to support that lifestyle.

8

Financing Your NewLife

John Trauth

All progress is based on the universal innate desire on the part of every living organism to live beyond its income.

—SAMUEL BUTLER, AUTHOR

Your dreams are now taking shape. But is the life that you have envisioned for yourself financially feasible? Will you have enough money to pay for your new lifestyle? What assets should you tap first? Will your money last?

Actually, you may have more resources than you think. This chapter will help you think strategically about your financial situation in light of the NewLife you are planning for yourself in retirement.

There are a large number of excellent financial-planning books available that focus on retirement. We have provided a list of some of the ones we like in the "Resources." Our intent is not to repeat the detailed information in these publications. Instead, we will provide you with some basic tools that will enable you to determine, in general terms, whether what you are planning to do in your NewLife is financially realistic.

The purpose of this chapter is to help answer the following questions:

1. How much money will I need to support my NewLife lifestyle, and where will it come from?
2. How can I be reasonably sure that it will last for the rest of my life?
3. How do I make it happen?

In the process of answering these questions, you may find that it is necessary to modify some of your NewLife plans, based on the realities of your financial situation. This process will again give you the opportunity to revisit your priorities and ask yourself what is really important. At the end of the NewLife Master Planning process, you need to feel comfortable with both what you are going to do and how you are going to do it from every angle: psychological, interpersonal, strategic, and financial.

How Much Money Will I Need and Where Will It Come From?

Financial planners will tell you that the average retiree needs approximately 80 percent of his or her preretirement after-tax income in retirement. Unless you radically change your lifestyle or move to another country where the dollar is still strong and the living is cheap and easy, 80 percent is probably a pretty good estimate. You will probably spend more in the early retirement years and less later.* But 80 percent is a good overall estimate.

---

*Financial planners will tell you that you may spend more in early retirement, when you are traveling and more active, and less later on, presuming, of course, that you have decent health insurance.

With this in mind, let's begin to figure out how much your NewLife will cost. We will begin with an example of someone facing this challenge. He is our friend Ken from Chapter 7, a professional consultant in practice as a sole practitioner in San Francisco. He lives in a high-cost region, makes a good living, and has multiple sources of income and expenses. I have chosen Ken because his situation is somewhat complex in order to illustrate a number of options. Your situation may be very different. You may just have a pension plan and Social Security, which will make these exercises easier and, if so, you can skip most of this chapter. Or you may have much more. The point is to show you an example of how one person might reorganize his or her finances in retirement, to help you understand the options and possible methodology so you can do this for yourself.

Here's a summary of Ken's OldLife situation, starting with his sources of income. He earns income from his consulting practice. In addition, he owns the small office building where he has his office and rents out three other spaces, which provides him with rental income as well as investment property deductions. His wife works part-time on her hobby, making stained glass windows, which also generates some income. Finally, he has written a book about the industry in which he consults which is in its second printing and is providing some royalty income, but the amount and longevity of this income is uncertain.

He also has ongoing expenses. Like everyone else, he and his wife have personal living expenses (food, clothing, transportation, entertainment, and so on.). His son is married and has a good job, so Ken has no further financial obligations there. He has two mortgages, one on his house (with ten years to run) and another on his office (with fourteen years to run).

He has a second home in the mountains near Lake Tahoe that he inherited from his parents and owns free and clear but of course he has some maintenance expenses. In fact, he has ongoing maintenance expenses and property taxes associated with his three properties. He has not rented it in the past, but he could if necessary. He pays medical insurance premiums for his wife and himself, which will reduce somewhat in five years when he is eligible for Medicare. He has travel expenses associated with two vacation trips a year, a short one at Christmas and a long one in the summer when he spends each August with his family in their mountain home. And he has two additional expenses, his contributions to his retirement plan, in his case, a Keogh defined-benefit plan, and his contributions to Social Security.

Figure 8.1 shows how his OldLife is structured financially.

Ken's immediate NewLife plan is to cut back his billable hours by 40 percent, retaining only his best clients and referring the others to his colleagues, while at the same time raising his hourly rates by 20 percent, which he thinks he can do with his best clients. This plan will give him more time to pursue his other interests, while still generating enough income to fund the majority of his anticipated NewLife expenses. He also has scheduled a rent increase of 5 percent for the three tenants in his office building. He plans to rent his second home for nine months a year to a professor and his family at Sierra College, located nearby. The professor travels during the summer, so Ken and his family can continue to spend the month of August there. This turns the second home from a use of his income to a source of his retirement funds because the rent will more than offset its maintenance costs and property taxes.

Figure 8.1   **Ken's OldLife Sources and Uses Chart**

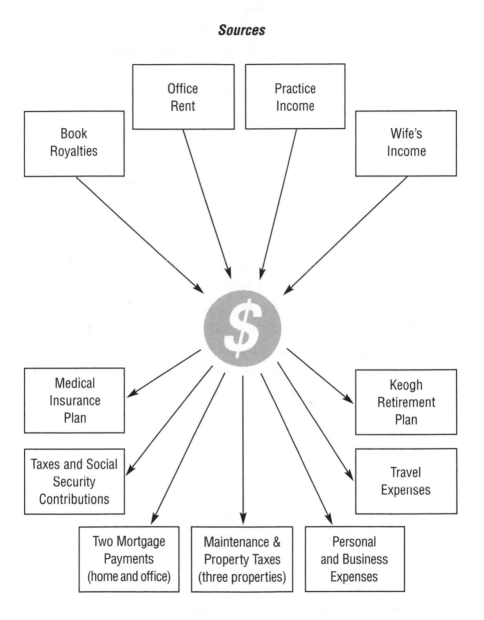

Sources

Book Royalties

Office Rent

Practice Income

Wife's Income

$

Medical Insurance Plan

Keogh Retirement Plan

Taxes and Social Security Contributions

Travel Expenses

Two Mortgage Payments (home and office)

Maintenance & Property Taxes (three properties)

Personal and Business Expenses

Uses

That is Ken's short-term NewLife plan. Longer term, in about five years, he plans to stop working entirely or to cut back to minimal hours. At that point, he plans to start taking his Social Security, so his contributions cease and this becomes a new source. He also plans to sell his office building and move his office into his home. This will give him a chunk of equity (after capital gains taxes) to invest, which will help fund his early retirement years so that he doesn't have to tap his tax-sheltered funds until later when they can change from a use to another new source.

Figure 8.2 shows the restructuring on Ken's sources and uses statement for his short-term NewLife Plan. Note that his second home has moved from the bottom of the chart (eliminating a use of income) to the top (a new source of income). In five years, when he implements his long-term plan, he will add Social Security as a new source. He will also add another new income source, investment income resulting from investing the proceeds of the sale of his office building. At the bottom of the chart, he will eliminate one of his mortgages and reduce his property maintenance expenses, because he no longer has the office building maintenance responsibilities. These new sources of income are shown on the chart as dotted lines because they will happen later.

Figure 8.3 shows Ken's OldLife financial cash flow and the changes that will happen as a result of his short-term decisions. His practice income is reduced by 28 percent (after reducing his billable hours by 40 percent but increasing his hourly rate by 20 percent). His office rent income increases 5 percent based on the rent increase. His wife plans to continue her part-time work and believes that she can increase her prices somewhat for her stained glass work, so that income increases marginally. The book income continues, but it will

Figure 8.2 **Ken's NewLife Sources and Uses Chart: Short-Term Plan (Five Years)**

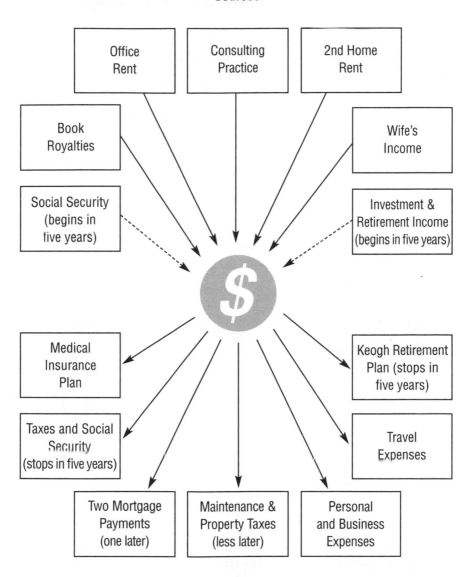

Sources

Office Rent

Consulting Practice

2nd Home Rent

Book Royalties

Wife's Income

Social Security (begins in five years)

Investment & Retirement Income (begins in five years)

Medical Insurance Plan

Keogh Retirement Plan (stops in five years)

Taxes and Social Security (stops in five years)

Travel Expenses

Two Mortgage Payments (one later)

Maintenance & Property Taxes (less later)

Personal and Business Expenses

Uses

Figure 8.3 **Ken's Cash Flow Projections: OldLife and NewLife**

Category	OldLife	NewLife
Income:		
Consulting Practice	$ 170,000	$122,000
Office Rent	$ 43,200	$ 45,360
Wife's Income	$ 12,000	$14,000
Book Royalties	$ 5,000	$ 3,000
2nd Home Rent	-0-	$ 13,500
Investment Income	-0-	-0-
Social Security		
Other		
Total Income:	$ 230,200	$ 197,860
Expenses:		
Business Expenses*	$ 22,000	$ 15,000
Medical Insurance	$ 9,000	$ 9,500
Property Maintenance	$ 36,000	$ 37,000
Food and Personal	$ 50,000	$ 52,000
Personal Travel	$ 20,000	$ 21,000
Mortgages	$ 37,200	$ 37,200
Keogh Contribution	$ 20,000	$ 13,000
Taxes/Social Security	$ 16,000	$ 9,000
Other		
Total Expenses:	$ 210,000	$ 193,700
Cash Remainder**	$ 20,000	$ 4,160

*Business expenses associated with Ken's professional practice (office supplies, equipment, depreciation, conferences, and travel, etc.)
**For savings, investments, or reallocation to above categories

likely diminish gradually and last only a few more years, so he can't count on that for the long term.

Look at what happens to his expenses. Working 60 percent of the time will reduce his business expenses. He still has two mortgages to pay until he implements his five-year plan and sells his office building. He still has his medical expenses, which increase slightly, but his portion is still deductible against his practice income. His travel and leisure expenses will not increase very much because he plans to use the extra time not working to relax at home and reread his favorite classic Great Books collection. And finally, because his total sources of income are more than sufficient to cover his total expenses, he will be able to continue to contribute to his defined benefit pension plan.

Let's now suppose that Ken's sources of income were *not* sufficient to cover his NewLife expenses. What are his options? Here are some examples:

- Sell the office building now, rather than later, with an agreement to lease back his space for five years. This strategy eliminates one of his mortgages now and cashes in his equity in the building, which he can then invest to provide another source of income to fund his NewLife.
- Use some of his new free time to help his wife expand and grow her part-time stained glass window business to generate more income.
- Teach courses two nights a week in his professional specialty at the local university.
- Turn his retirement plan from an expense to another source of income to cover whatever deficit remains.

- Later on, when he stops working entirely or when it makes sense from a tax perspective, he can add in Social Security to the equation.

There could be other options, such as write another book or turn a hobby into a business, but you get the idea.

Now it is time to do this for yourself. As I mentioned earlier, your situation may be more or less complicated than Ken's, and you may have other, entirely different options, such as pension income or stock options. But follow the same process.

Begin with filling out the Sources and Uses Chart in Figure 8.4 using information based on your OldLife. Do this in pencil. When you have completed the chart, fill in the first column of the table in Figure 8.5 with the financial information from your OldLife, using your current annual data.

Now, think about how you plan to reorganize your sources and uses to support your NewLife. Think about what uses you can turn into sources. Then get out your pencil and eraser and go back to your Sources and Uses Chart in Figure 8.4 and move those around.

Next, estimate how this rearrangement will affect your NewLife finances and fill in the second column of the table in Figure 8.5 with estimates of your NewLife income* and expenses. We have included common categories, but you may need to add in your own. If your life is complicated and the table is too small, make your own. To make realistic estimates, look at your recent tax returns, bank statements, and credit card charges to refresh your memory about where your money is coming from and where it is going. Build in some extra money, because there will always be some unanticipated expenses.

---

*Technically, if you are spending after-tax dollars, this is not "income" but rather a revenue source.

Figure 8.4 ***My OldLife to NewLife Sources and Uses Chart***

Sources

Uses

Figure 8.5 *My Cash Flows Projections: OldLife and NewLife*

Category	OldLife	NewLife
Income:		
Professional Income	$	$
Royalties	$	$
Investment Income	$	$
Social Security	$	$
Other	$	$
Other	$	$
Other	$	$
Total Income:	$	$
Expenses:		
Professional Expenses	$	$
Medical Insurance	$	$
Property Maintenance	$	$
Personal Living Expenses	$	$
Travel	$	$
Mortgage(s)	$	$
Retirement Contribution	$	$
Taxes/Social Security	$	$
Other	$	$
Total Expenses:	$	$
Cash Remainder*	$	$

*For savings, investments, or reallocation to above categories

As a reality check, ask yourself how close you are to the 80 percent estimate. If you are way off, what is the reason? Are you forgetting something?

After you have finished, take a look at the bottom line, "Cash Remainder," of your NewLife projections. What does this tell you? Can you live with this number and the implications? If not, go back and make adjustments. Think of any reduction in this number, from your OldLife to your NewLife, as "buying back your time" to invest in your future. And think also of the returns it will pay in terms of your new lifestyle. Is the investment worth the return? If so, great! If not, go back and make corrections until you feel that the investment more than justifies the return.

How to Be Sure Your Money Will Last

If you are deciding not to work in retirement, not to move, not sell anything, and just start drawing your company pension and Social Security, the above exercises will be simple. But easy or not, almost everyone except the very wealthy will be wondering how to be sure that their money will last. Here is how to get the best answer to that question.

Working part-time in early retirement helps enormously. An analysis conducted by Merrill Lynch estimates that earning 40 percent of your previous salary for the first five years after retirement is likely to add 30 percent to the balance of your retirement portfolio when you retire, which will provide additional funds to support your lifestyle for your later years. Keeping productive through part-time work makes a *big* difference for two reasons:

- It extends the period during which you don't have to tap your tax-sheltered retirement funds (or, if you do, by not as much).
- It gives the money in your tax-sheltered retirement portfolio more time to grow before you start drawing from it.

Financial-Planning Programs

No load and low-cost mutual funds, like Vanguard and Fidelity, and full-service brokerage houses like Merrill Lynch offer free or moderately priced financial-planning programs for retirement that are based on sophisticated simulation models. You provide the personal information for yourself and your spouse/partner (age, health, life expectancy, financial assets, and other information), and they run the simulation and help you interpret the results. The questions also ask you about your part-time work plans and other potential sources of income and even probe you about your likely future significant purchases, such as a new car, a new roof for your home, and so on. You can even run some of these programs online.

For example, Fidelity's program is based on "Monte Carlo" simulations that take into account the possibility of market corrections early in the retirement years. This is important, as anyone who retired in 1973 or 1999 can tell you, because major corrections occurred in the following years and the market did not fully recover for a long time. The investment portfolios of many people who retired in the early seventies never completely recovered from these significant early losses and, as a consequence, their retirement lifestyle was permanently compromised. We will show you how to minimize the possibility of this happening to you later in this chapter.

The models will give you good estimates about how long your money will last. As circumstances change, you can go back and change some of your earlier assumptions to see how this changes the results.

Structuring Your Investments

How you structure your investments in your retirement accounts will also determine how long your money is likely to last. Not surprisingly, the simulation models take asset allocation into account. Generally, when you were younger, you could invest more aggressively because you had many years to ride out market corrections, with the high likelihood of a long-term positive trend. Now you have less time to do this and cannot afford significant early portfolio losses, so you will need to be more conservative.

A good way to minimize the potential problem of an early market correction decimating your retirement portfolio is to practice what I call "double diversification." That is to say, diversify both within and among asset classes.

Here is a personal example to illustrate how this is done. Years ago, I worked for the San Francisco Foundation, the largest community foundation in the San Francisco Bay Area. Recently, my wife and I set up a donor-advised fund there. Donor-advised funds are funds that you contribute to a foundation (which gives you an immediate charitable deduction); the foundation holds the funds and invests them while you decide how and when they will be granted to worthy nonprofit organizations of your choosing. Obviously, you don't want to make a donation to a foundation with high administrative expenses nor one that is not likely to invest your funds prudently.

I attend the San Francisco Foundation's annual meetings where the foundation reports on its investment strategy for its endowment and its recent performance. The foundation's investment committee includes several of the city's financial luminaries who know their stuff. They have designed an investment strategy with the objective of participating in the market's upside (to retain the purchasing power of their future grants) while also minimizing the potential losses. To say it another way, they are willing to take some measured risk to participate in market gains, while at the same time protecting the portfolio from major losses. When I heard that strategy, it sounded very much like the strategy I wanted to use with my retirement money, so I adopted it for my retirement portfolio.

The asset classes and the percentages the Foundation's investment committee recently used are as follows:

Type	Percentage	Description
US Large Cap Equities	34%	Largest US corporations
US Mid Cap Equities	11%	Medium-sized US corporations
US Small Cap Equities	14%	Smaller US corporations
International Equities	12%	Companies in other countries
High-Yield Fixed Income	6%	Higher-risk bonds
Absolute Return	7.5%	Guaranteed return instruments
Fixed Income	15.5%	Bonds, CDs and equivalents

Each year, they make minor adjustments in the percentages, but you can be quite comfortable using these figures. Splitting your investments among these asset classes is the first level of diversification. (This may sound complicated, but I will show you an easy way to do it.)

The second level of diversification is to take each of these asset classes and spread your investments among a significant number of companies. If you are a $400 million operation, like the San Francisco Foundation, you can hire money market managers to do this for you and potentially beat the indexes. If you are very wealthy, you can do the same. If you are not, you can do what I do, which is to buy index funds for each of these categories. Index funds give you the broadest diversification possible for the lowest possible cost, particularly if you use low-cost mutual fund companies, but full-service brokerage houses also offer equivalent investments. If you already have a trusted advisor, I recommend that you work with that person to implement this strategy.

To give you one example of how this works, in Figure 8.6 I have matched the asset classes and percentages with equivalent Vanguard indexes. Fidelity and many other mutual fund and full-service brokerage houses like Merrill Lynch have equivalent index funds you could also use.

Some financial advisors will argue that this suggested allocation represents too high a concentration in equities for people about to retire because of the increased volatility associated with stocks. However, by using double diversification, including equities in foreign companies, that volatility is reduced. Nevertheless, it is a good idea to reduce the percentage in equities (the first four categories) as you get older. Why? Because your life expectancy gets shorter as you age, reducing volatility

Figure 8.6   **_Possible Asset Allocation Plan_**

Asset Class	Percentage	Equivalent Vanguard Fund
US Large Cap Equities	34%	Vanguard 500 Index
US Mid Cap Equities	11%	Vanguard Mid Cap Index
US Small Cap Equities	14%	Vanguard Small Cap Index
International Equities	12%	Vanguard Int'l Growth Fund
High-Yield Fixed Income	6%	Vanguard High Yield Corporate Bond Fund
Absolute Return	7.5%	Vanguard Inflation Protected Securities Fund
Fixed Income	15.5%	Vanguard Total Bond Market Index (alternative is Intermdiate Term Corporate Bond Fund*)

*To reduce taxes for those with other significant income outside of retirement accounts, part or all of the Total Bond Market Index might be replaced with a municipal income fund, perhaps specific to the state of residence. One example would be a state-specific Fidelity Municipal Income fund for your state of residence.

is a good strategy so that a few bad years in the stock market will not permanently affect your retirement assets and compromise your future lifestyle. For example, you might start your retirement with the above allocation, presuming that you also plan to work part-time, and gradually reduce the equities concentration so that, by age 75, or when you stop working entirely, you have equal proportions of equities and fixed income investments (50 percent each). If you want more detailed information, there are many good books on investing in retirement, some of which are listed in "Resources."

Most financial planners also recommend that you maintain a portion of your assets in cash. A minimum of a six-month reserve (sometimes called an "emergency fund") is usually suggested, but you can certainly choose a higher number if you want more stability and less risk in your portfolio. If you have adequate cash outside of your retirement accounts, you can keep your retirement accounts fully invested. However, if your retirement accounts are all of the assets that you have, then you will need to add a cash equivalent asset, like a money market fund or very short-term bank CDs (certificates of deposit), to the above allocations. Decide whether it makes sense to keep a cash position in your retirement portfolio and, if so, add that category and percentage, reducing the other percentages proportionally. I would not recommend exceeding 15 percent of your portfolio in cash unless your account is very, very small—in which case, you have other problems to worry about.

By following this strategy of double diversification, you protect yourself from major market corrections while giving yourself the opportunity to participate in the market's upside. For example, if you had implemented this strategy starting in early 1998, without cash equivalents and maintaining the allocations shown in Figure 8.6, you would have participated in 65 percent of the market's gains and only 12 percent of its losses between 1998 and the end of 2004, a time when many people lost their shirts during the dot-com collapse and subsequent market correction.

In summary, if you run the simulations and invest using double diversification, you will know with a reasonable amount of certainty that your money will last for the amount of time that the model says it will. Now, all you have to do is last that long yourself!

How to Make It Happen Financially

Let's say that you have completed all of your plans and you are now ready to put your financial retirement plan into effect. How do you do it?

Step 1: Restructure Your Sources and Uses

By now, you should have decided how to restructure your sources and uses of income to support your NewLife and are prepared to make those adjustments. As soon as you are ready to kick off your NewLife (or perhaps several months beforehand), it is time to implement those plans.

Step 2: Spend Your Non-Tax-Sheltered Funds First

Any income needs that you have that result from reducing or stopping work should first be funded from your non-tax-sheltered investments. These are your assets that are not in your IRAs, Roth IRAs, 401(k)s, 403(b)s, SEPs, and other retirement accounts. Only draw upon your retirement resources when you have spent your non-tax-sheltered funds.

Why? Because you have already paid taxes on these funds, so it makes sense to use them first.* Because you postponed taxation on your retirement fund contributions, you will incur a tax liability when you withdraw them. Meanwhile, they grow tax-free. Leave them there until you absolutely need them.

---

*Except for your ROTH accounts, which are made with after-tax contributions. You should withdraw them last since they are not subject to the mandatory withdrawal requirements that begin at age seventy for your other tax-sheltered accounts. There are also estate-planning advantages to this strategy. Discuss this with your financial planner and/or tax advisor.

Step 3: Determine the Best Time to Start Taking Social Security

In general, if you are planning to stop working entirely, and you are sixty-two or older or disabled, and you need the additional income, it probably makes sense to start taking Social Security immediately. Unless you significantly exceed your life expectancy, the extra Social Security payments in the early years probably means that you will get more Social Security income over your total remaining lifetime than if you wait for somewhat higher monthly payments later.

However, if you will continue to have earned income, you will be penalized rather severely. For example, if you earn more than $12,000 a year, you will currently be taxed $1 for every $2 of Social Security you receive. If you plan to continue to have earned income, particularly in your early retirement years, it may make sense to wait. When you receive your annual Social Security statement, read it carefully to determine what your benefits will be at certain ages, and factor that into your analysis. After you reach your "full retirement age," (sixty-five years and six months for those born in 1940, and gradually rising to sixty-seven for those born in 1960 and later), you can earn as much as you like without having your Social Security benefits penalized.

Step 4: Keep Early Retirement Fund Withdrawals to 4 Percent

When you do have to draw on your retirement savings, plan to withdraw only 4 percent of your total retirement assets in the first year (and increase that amount annually by the rate of inflation). This will help insure that the funds will last for the rest of your life. The simulation models take your planned withdrawal rates into account in projecting how long your money will last.

Go back to your calculations of your retirement income. After taking into account your Social Security and your other sources of income, were you planning to withdraw more than 4 percent of your retirement savings to fund your NewLife in the early years? If you were, you may need to reconsider and make some adjustments in your NewLife plan.

How much money will you need?

If you have no company pension and you are planning on living on your 401(k) or similar plan assets combined with Social Security, your retirement assets better be quite substantial. You can calculate just how much by using the following formula:

Amount of yearly income desired from retirement portfolio = Size of retirement fund ÷ .04

For example, after tapping other sources, if you were counting on withdrawing $5,000 a month from your retirement fund, this would be $60,000 a year, which means that you would need to have $60,000/.04, or $1,500,000, in your retirement account at the time you retire. And remember that you are going to owe taxes on that $60,000.

For many people, this is a "whoops" moment. Maybe you are fine, but maybe you are not even close. If you are in the latter category, don't despair. You have a number of options. Most retirees with a NewLife Master Plan will want to work part-time in early retirement and, as we said before, this can make a *big* difference financially. Of course, you can also adjust your NewLife plans and priorities and rethink the sources and uses of your postretirement income. We intentionally wanted you to make your NewLife plans before you did the financial calculations. Now you can figure out what is really important to you and set your sights on that.

If you are not using the simulation models, the 4 percent rule is still a good rule to follow. Also, if you are not using the models, do not base your financial-planning assumptions on your "average lifespan." If you know you have a terminal illness and can estimate your remaining time with reasonable accuracy, that's one thing. But basing your projections on the average remaining life expectancy for someone of your age is not a good idea. Approximately half of the people live longer than the average (and the rest die sooner). Be optimistic. If you are in good health and plan to continue to exercise and eat well, you will have a long time ahead of you—which is why it is so important to plan well for this phase of your life. If your money has to support two of you, you need to consider the probability that one of you will outlive the other. The simulation models take all of this and other things you probably haven't thought of into account, which is why it is so helpful to use them.

If it all still isn't adding up, here is one fallback alternative: a reverse mortgage. It doesn't work for everyone but might work for you if you own your home, have substantial equity in it, and plan to continue to live there for the foreseeable future.

A reverse mortgage allows you to tap the equity in your home, and it can provide you with a monthly source of essentially tax-free income. I worked for the company that pioneered this program in the early 1980s in Marin County, just north of San Francisco. To use this option effectively, you should have little or no remaining mortgage. And if there is any possibility that you might want to move later on, it may not make sense because there are significant origination costs and an on-going requirement that your house remain your primary residence. But if you meet these conditions, a reverse mortgage might be another way to generate additional monthly income. Some financial advisors recommend this as a way to postpone drawing on your retirement savings in the early retirement years, or at least not drawing as much. How much you can withdraw each month from a reverse mortgage depends on a number of factors, including your age, prevailing interest rates, loan costs, estimated equity in your home, whether or not your loan is FHA-insured, and when and for how long you want the income. When you have tapped the eligible equity (assume between 40 percent and 50 percent of your total equity), the payments stop* but you can continue to live in your home and will not have to pay back the balance during your lifetime. Your heirs will settle the loan from your estate. Because there are many variations of reverse mortgages and payment options, it is a complicated decision. For more information, advice, and guidance, contact the AARP Foundation's Reverse Mortgage Education Project (800-209-8085); aarp.org/revmort. After AARP, another source for advice and information is the nonprofit National Center for Home Equity Conversion (reverse.org). A list of qualified lenders can be found at the National Reverse Mortgage Lenders Association site (reversemortgage.org).

Step 5: Make the Withdrawals Automatic

If you are investing your retirement savings in mutual funds, this is easy. Just tell your mutual fund company what monthly income you want and instruct them to sell the required

---

*Some lenders will allow a reappraisal at a later date and, if your home has continued to appreciate, the payments may be extended, but this is not guaranteed.

number of shares from certain funds and send you a check each month at a certain date. They are set up to do this. Full-service brokers can obviously do the same thing, but, in this case, watch out for commissions that could eat into your retirement assets. If you have your retirement funds invested in stocks and bonds with a full-service broker, you may instead want to cash out six months of living expenses at a time to keep the transaction fees reasonable.

Step 6: Rebalance Your Portfolio Every Six Months

Rebalancing your portfolio is a good rule even if you are not yet withdrawing funds from your retirement account, because different asset classes will perform differently over time. If you have decided on your asset category mix and practiced double diversification, you will still need to rebalance your retirement portfolio even if you are not withdrawing funds. It is easy to forget to do this. Unless you trade the market actively and constantly rebalance your portfolio, it is good to pick a six-month schedule and stay on that schedule. I find that I have time in the holiday period between Christmas and New Year's Day and also at the beginning of summer, so I do my rebalancing in late December and at the end of June each year. You could choose your birthday and another significant holiday six months later. Or put the date in your agenda or online calendar. Do whatever works for you. Just establish a system and stick with it. This way, you will remember to do it.

These are the six steps to take to put your retirement income plan into effect to support your NewLife. I will offer one further suggestion. I am a fan of long-term care insurance. Medical policies today generally do not cover long-term care, and this coverage is sold as a separate policy by insurance companies. Estimates are that 40 percent of people over age sixty-five will spend some time in a long-term care facility. And a long illness requiring long-term care can be financially devastating. The earlier you buy long-term care insurance, the lower the monthly premiums. You can sometimes opt for a constant premium that is higher initially but doesn't increase as you get older. Shop for it as you would shop for any other insurance product. Given the expense of health care in our country and the enormous costs associated with long-term care, think of a long-term care policy as an insurance policy for your retirement portfolio, too.

This chapter has given you the basics about how to finance your NewLife. Further issues, such as life insurance, annuities, estate planning, and other related aspects of retirement planning and investing are complicated subjects, and there are already many good books that deal with them (some are listed in the "Resources" section). Go into as much detail as you want on this subject, but keep in mind the *Your Retirement, Your Way* process: focus first on determining the NewLife you want, and *then* figure out how to finance it—rather than the other way around.

As you continue in the coming chapters to refine your NewLife Master Plan, remember the words that Robert Kennedy spoke often as he traveled around this great nation: "Some men see things as they are and ask 'Why?' I dream things that never were and ask 'Why not?'"

9

Planning Your Transition

John Trauth

It is not so much that we are afraid of change—or so in love with the way things are—it's the place in between that we fear. It's kind of like being between trapezes. It's Linus when his blanket is in the drier. There's nothing to hold on to.

—MARILYN FERGUSON,
AUTHOR, POET

By now, you have your vision of your ideal retirement life, you have the other important people in your life on board with your plan, you have your NewLife road map, and you have a good idea about how you are going to finance your future life.

To make it all happen, to make it all real, you now need to plan your transition.

This may sound easy, but it might just be the hardest part. As discussed in Chapter 2, there are a lot of potential roadblocks, both operational and psychological, that can derail your plans. Remember "analysis paralysis"? The purpose of this chapter is to help you understand why you might be hesitating and realize that these symptoms are a common part of major life transitions, as well as to give you some tools to help you move forward.

LifeLaunch: A Passionate Guide to the Rest of Your Life, by Frederic M. Hudson and Pamela D. McLean, is a terrific resource on transitions. In our lives, we experience many transitions, with retirement being one of the major ones, and this book helps put them in perspective. Hudson and McLean believe that "the secret to a resilient life in our kind of world is knowing how to recycle yourself, over and over, letting go of what is no longer you, taking on new strengths, and shaping new chapters for your life, guided by your own emerging vision." They explain that the "Personal Renewal Cycle" involves three elements:

- "Holding on" to what is valuable and working in your life, including activities you want to do more of
- "Letting go" of what is not working, is worn out, and doesn't belong in your future
- "Taking on" new skills, resources, attitudes, and activities for creating the next chapter in your life

After you have done these three things, it is time to "Move on" to your new life.

Sound familiar? This is essentially what you have done in the previous chapters. And now, with your NewLife clearly in your sights, the only thing remaining is to "Just Do It!" Right?

Not so fast. After all, knowing the plan and making it happen are two very different things.

Create Your Transition Timetable

Before you go public with your plans, create a specific timetable for your transition. So get out your agenda or planner and answer, for yourself first, the following questions:

1. What is the ideal date for me to officially "retire" from my OldLife? Mark this date on your calendar. Wow—you did it!
2. What do I need to finish between now and then to feel that I have completed my existing commitments in my OldLife? What work am I doing that only I can finish? What work can I turn over to others? Will I need to train them? If so, how long will it take?
3. What financial restructuring do I need to do between now and my retirement date so that I am financially ready to assume my NewLife?
4. What else do I need to do to be prepared to launch my NewLife? Are there others from whom I need buy-in and support? Is there training or education that I need for the next phase? Are there other arrangements that are critical to moving forward that need to be in place?
5. Are my answers to questions 2, 3, and 4 consistent with the date I set in question 1? If not, what adjustment(s) should I make? (Use this exercise as a way to design a realistic transition plan, not as a way to procrastinate. Maybe you can even do it even sooner than you thought!)

Set specific target dates by which you hope to accomplish the tasks you have identified above. For example, when can you wrap up that major research project, finish the client report, complete your last consultation, or identify your referrals? If you are planning to start a new part-time business, you may want to develop your business plan and arrange the line of credit you will need now, while you are fully employed, because it will be more difficult to get it approved once you are no longer employed full-time. Put these estimated completion dates on your calendar as well.

Once you have entered these dates in your calendar, create your own Gantt Chart, or time line chart. Figure 9.1 shows the format, with only the general items discussed above. Your chart should be much more detailed than this one. Here we have used months to show the passage of time in anticipation that the transition would take six months. You may elect to use weeks or even days. Use as many columns and rows as necessary. Be very specific, and write the beginning and ending dates for each activity under the bold lines.

Your transition should be starting to feel more real.

The next thing you need to do is to share and validate your transition plans with your spouse or partner, your family, and any other significant people in your private life whose advice you value, particularly those who you plan to involve in your NewLife. Follow the same process you used in Chapter 6 when you shared and validated your dreams with them. Talk over your transition plans. Share with them the dates you have set for yourself. Get their feedback. Make whatever adjustments you feel are appropriate. If you have disagreements with the key people in your life, seek resolution through discussion and, if necessary, compromise. But insist on establishing specific dates for each of your intended actions. It is OK if the ultimate retirement date is three months, six months, a year, or even longer out. If, after your consultations

Figure 9.1   ***NewLife Transition Chart***

Activity	Mo 1	Mo 2	Mo 3	Mo 4	Mo 5	Mo 6
1. Establish Date; Develop Timetable	▓▓▓ 1/1–31/YR					
2. Get Buy-in	▓▓▓ 1/15–2/15/YR					
3. Inform Boss		X 2/02/YR				
4. Complete Work Only I Can Do		▓▓▓ 2/1/YR	▓▓▓	▓▓▓ 4/30/YR		
5. Train Others to Assume Work			▓▓▓ 3/1/YR	▓▓▓	▓▓▓ 5/30/YR	
6. Perform Financial Restructuring				▓▓▓ 4/10/YR	▓▓▓ 5/30/YR	
7. Prepare for NewLife (training, etc.)				▓▓▓ 4/1/YR	▓▓▓	▓▓▓ 6/30/YR
8. Retirement Party!						X ! 6/29/YR

with your loved ones, you decide to change that date, go back and change the other transition dates. At the end of the exercise, those closest to you should be supportive of your plan.

This process will also make your retirement feel *even more real*! You may even be thinking, "Good grief! This is actually going to happen!"

Now, armed with the support and buy-in of your family and friends, you are ready to approach your employer and break the news.* Set this up carefully. Prepare in advance. Start by saying, "Boss, I've got something important I want to discuss with you. When can we find some time in the near future to get together?" Suggest how much time you need, probably at least a half hour or more for the initial meeting. Be prepared if he or she says, "How about right now?" If this happens, respond by saying, "That would be great, as long as we could have at least XX minutes of uninterrupted time." This way, you are informing him or her of the importance of the conversation and setting the parameters for the discussion.

Be prepared to discuss not only your decision and retirement date but also to talk through the details of your transition. What work will you complete yourself? Who will you identify/hire/train to take over the rest? How long will each transitional activity take? If you are proposing to continue working part-time for the same employer after your retirement date, explain your proposal and the time parameters associated with it. For example, you might propose to continue to work at a 50 percent level for one or two years after your retirement, perhaps on a consulting or contract basis, with an annual review of how the situation is working for both of you. Don't forget to discuss compensation and benefits. Build in an early termination clause in case the situation is not working for either of you. Your discussion will demonstrate that you have thought a lot about your decision, that you are a responsible and trustworthy person, that you care

_____

*Obviously, if you are an individual professional or self-employed, you don't have a "boss," but you may need to use a similar process to determine how you will inform your patients, clients, contractors, and so on.

about your employer and company, and that you want the transition to be as smooth as possible.

But remember also that you are doing this primarily for yourself. You might feel guilty when you say "no" to someone. But remember that if you say "yes" to your boss who wants you to continue to work, at the same time you are saying "no" to yourself, your family, and your NewLife. The time management exercises you did in Chapter 5 and refined in Chapter 7 demonstrated clearly the tradeoffs you make in life. You can't have your NewLife until you leave your OldLife. There truly can't be a beginning before there is an ending. As Anaïs Nin said, "Life shrinks or expands in proportion to one's courage." That is why you need to embrace change and have the courage to begin your transition to retirement. Go back now and reread your NewLife vision statement. Think of it as a magnet, drawing you forward.

Take a Break!

Now that you have completed the previous tasks and have established your retirement date, consider adding in some time off between your OldLife and your NewLife. It will be difficult to have the retirement party on Friday afternoon, go home, and then not go to work on Monday. If you have done your work well in the earlier chapters, you should feel anxious to get started. That's great. But a little vacation (or a big one) can be very effective in helping you with the transition because you will have something more immediate and very pleasurable to look forward to. Have you always wanted to visit Costa Rica? Surf in Hawaii? Find and connect with lost relatives? Do it! You've earned it! Besides, this is an excellent time to do it. A vacation is a positive stimulus that you can couple with your retirement party, and, by providing an immediate and positive distraction, it will take some of the pressure off the enormity of the decision you are making. More importantly, it will allow you to recharge your batteries. Consciously or unconsciously, you will be thinking about your NewLife and internally processing and reprocessing how you will make it all come about. You will most likely come home even more energized and ready to begin this next phase of your life.

In Chapter 1, I told you that, immediately after I retired, my wife and I flew to France and lived there for a year. Looking back, that was an excellent decision. The break with my OldLife was complete. Had I stayed in San Francisco, my office would have been calling me frequently with questions about this and that. Being in a time zone nine hours away (or on the beach in Costa Rica, or traveling in Asia, or wherever) helps to make that break complete. It is better for you and, ultimately, better for those who have to assume your responsibilities, because they have no other choice.

Anticipating and Channeling Stress

Even if you fully embrace change and have sufficient courage to begin the journey to your NewLife, there will be stress involved. Have the important people in your life fully bought in to your plan? Has your boss reacted positively to your decision and your proposed timetable? Will you be able to meet the timetable you have set for yourself? Will your financial resources be adequate to sustain your NewLife? Have unforeseen problems arisen?

That this time will be stressful is certain, because all transitions involve stress. The important thing is how you handle the stress. If you lie in bed sleepless every night, pondering the possible outcomes of your intended actions, you will internalize your stress, make yourself tense and nervous, and potentially harm your health. To avoid these potential negatives, you may just decide that it is all too much and that it is easier to just continue working full-time.

Don't give in to this temptation. The French philosopher Montaigne once reflected, "My life has been full of terrible misfortunes, most of which never happened."

So if you really want to move forward, put these negative thoughts aside and learn how to channel your stress into positive channels. In classes on public speaking, we are taught that stress is a natural phenomenon when speaking before an audience. Actors and actresses, even the best ones, get nervous before a performance. The trick is to recognize that stress is normal in these circumstances and to channel that stress into the activity at hand in a positive manner to improve your performance. Use that extra adrenalin for good purposes rather than bad. Whereas the transition to retirement is a longer process than these examples illustrate, each transitional activity will have stress associated with it. In each instance, channel your stress into positive energy to enhance your performance.

Avoiding Cynicism

In this complicated world, with the tremendous flow of information, much of it negative, it can be easy to become cynical—not just about the world around but also about yourself and your ability to create positive change. If this happens, and you find that enthusiasm for moving forward with your transition is diminishing, remind yourself that your life is ultimately under your own control. Don't internalize and take personally what you can't control. As they often teach in stress management courses, "You are doing it to yourself; therefore, you can stop doing it to yourself and eliminate the consequences." In *LifeLaunch,* Frederic M. Hudson and Pamela D. McLean assert that, if you are to be successful in managing your life, "You can't afford to be cynical; you have to be cautiously optimistic to trust in your future, to live your dream, and to manage your plans."

Respecting Your Values and Staying Value Driven

When you were young, your values were prescribed by your parents. As you grew older, you probably challenged some or all of those assumptions, experimented with different value sets, and finally created your own set of values. At preretirement age, you know who you are and, most likely, your values are well tested and secure. Respect them. It is great to try new things, to continually learn new stuff. But don't plan a NewLife that will be in conflict with your basic value system. You know who and what you care about and the causes you believe in. Review your NewLife plan now to make sure that you will be respecting your values and priorities, that your NewLife will be consistent with your life's purpose, and that you will not be creating internal conflicts for yourself. After all, the ultimate goal is happiness and fulfillment. The next three chapters will provide you with tools that will help you to manage your NewLife toward that goal.

Creating Your NewLife Master Plan Summary

John Trauth

I always wanted to be someone . . . , but I should have been more specific.

—LILY TOMLIN, ACTRESS, COMEDIAN

You have now completed the basic planning for your NewLife. You have completed the self-analysis process through the Birkman® personality profile and the memories exercises. You have created a vision for your NewLife. You have constructed your NewLife road map. You have analyzed your financial situation and determined what restructuring will be necessary to support your new lifestyle. You have gotten buy-in for your plans from those important to you who will be sharing your journey.

It is time now to put it all together on one page!

Several years ago, I met Jim Horan, who had written a book called *The One Page Business Plan*, which shows that you don't need a 250-page plan to succeed in business and that it is more important to think through the key issues carefully. To make the business plan useful, Jim has created a format for reducing it to one page. It works because it takes a complex subject and makes it simple. It forces you to focus on what is important. And it is easily understandable. Having everything on one page gives you the ability to focus on the essentials of the plan and put it into action. I now use *The One Page Business Plan* with all of my clients, and they are thrilled with the results.

You are now going to do something similar. You are going to create your NewLife Master Plan Summary. Your plan will help you summarize concisely what you have done so far in planning for your retirement and focus on the essentials of your NewLife Master Plan. It will also help you put it into action. It will be a reference point for you when you consider new opportunities, and it is easily updatable.

You may be saying, "This is impossible. I have done so much writing and planning in this book. How am I ever going to put this all on one page?" The beauty of a one-page summary format is that it forces you to simplify and prioritize. It makes you determine what is really important and what is less so.

The format for your one page NewLife Plan Summary is shown in Figure 10.1, presented initially on two pages, and the process for creating it will be described soon. When preparing your NewLife Plan Summary, review the material you have previously written and shorten it into very concise language. As you enter the material, cut out any unnecessary words and phrases and use abbreviations and symbols (like &, +, and =). Use italics and boldface to add emphasis.

In addition, enter the most important items first, and drop low priority items. This will help communicate your priorities to yourself and to anyone else reading your summary. It will also help you focus on what is important, and this focus will sharpen your vision of what you have to do to attain your NewLife goals.

Write Your NewLife Vision

On Figure 10.1, begin with entering your name, your age, and today's date. Then copy your NewLife vision statement from the end of Chapter 5. If you would like to make any changes to the vision statement, based on what you have learned from Chapters 6 through 9, do it now.

Summarize Your Self-Analysis

Now go back and summarize your self-analysis exercises. You already prepared that summary at the end of Chapter 3. Enter the essentials of that analysis in the next section of your NewLife Master Plan Summary, including your key interests, style, needs, and skills.

Next, refer to your work in Chapter 4, when you took the mini-Birkman® personality profile. Enter your Birkman® interest color, and then summarize what this means in a few words. For example, if your interest color is Blue, you might write in "creative, thoughtful, humanistic." If it is Green, you might write in "persuasive, promotional, group oriented." If your interest color is Red, you might write in "practical, objective, problem solving." For Yellow, you might write in "organized, predictable, detail oriented." If you prefer to use other, similar words, refer back to the list in Chapter 4, "Applying Your Symbols," for other suggestions. Select the words that best describe you.

Do the same thing for your Birkman® style color. For example, if your style color is Blue, you might write in "supportive, contemplative." If it is Green, you might use the words "outgoing, forceful." If you are a Red, you might say, "action-oriented, practical." And Yellows might describe themselves as "orderly, definitive, stable." Again, there are suggestions for

Figure 10.1   **My NewLife Plan Summary**

Name: _____ Age: _____ Date: _____

My NewLife Vision: _____

_____

_____

_____

_____

_____

My Self-Analysis Summary:

Key Interests: _____

Style: _____

Needs: _____

Skills: _____

Situations: _____

Birkman® Interest Color: _____ meaning _____

_____

Birkman® Style Color: _____ meaning _____

_____

My Key NewLife Goals:

1. _____

2. _____

3. _____

4. _____

5. _____

6. _____

My First-Year Strategies:

1. _____

2. _____

3. _____

4. _____

5. _____

6. _____

My First-Year Objectives and Completion Dates:

1. _____

2. _____

3. _____

4. _____

5. _____

6. _____

My First-Year Activities/Tasks:

• _____

• _____

• _____

• _____

• _____

• _____

other words in Chapter 4. Use the words that best describe you. The purpose of this summary is to remind you later on about your self-analysis exercises and what they meant.

Key NewLife Goals

Now, write in your key NewLife goals. You can choose one from each life category, if you wish (work, family, couple, friends, community, and personal), but I recommend that you choose the ones that are the most important to you, the ones that you prioritized in Chapter 6, and are the most likely to help you achieve your NewLife vision.

For example, if your most important goals in retirement relate to couple, family, and community, you may want to list only your goals in those categories. Think this through carefully, because the rest of your NewLife Plan Summary will then relate primarily to these goals.

First-Year Strategies and Objectives

You created both five-year and one-year strategies in Chapter 7 when you constructed your NewLife road map. However, your NewLife Master Plan Summary will concentrate only on your first-year strategies and objectives. If you want to, you can also create a Five-Year NewLife Plan Summary and include there your five-year strategies and objectives. But do this as an addition to, not as a replacement for this exercise. Why? Because the process of creating your NewLife Plan Summary will keep you focused on what you need to do *now* to move yourself forward in pursuit of your NewLife vision.

Enter your first-year strategies and objectives, but *only* the ones that relate to your key NewLife goals, which you have already entered on your NewLife Plan Summary. When you are done, you and anyone else reading your NewLife Plan Summary should be able to see how everything in your plan relates to everything else.

First-Year Activities and Tasks

In the next section, enter only the first-year activities and tasks that relate to the NewLife goals and strategies that you have already written. If there is a sequence to these activi- ties, write them in that sequence. For example, if you want to learn to play the piano, and you don't have one, you will need to buy or rent one first. Combine activities and tasks when possible. Thus, your tasks for a goal of "Learn to play the piano" might be "Buy piano, find teacher, and begin lessons 2x/week." (Your corresponding strategy for this goal which you listed previously under "Strategies," might read, "Find the best piano teacher from the Julliard School of Music list.")

Review for Consistency

You have filled in all of the categories on your NewLife Master Plan Summary. Read it now in its entirety, top to bottom, and then ask yourself the following questions:

- Am I creating a NewLife for myself that is consistent with who I am, based on my self-analysis summary? Does anything seem out of whack? In short, am I trying to do things that complement my interests, style, needs and skills? Is what I am planning to do consistent with my Birkman® results? Am I trying to change my personality rather than building on my strengths? (This is not to suggest that you not try something new. Remember the example in Chapter 1 of the successful businessman who, after retiring, became an unsuccessful actor and then a successful off-Broadway producer.)

- Are these really my top-priority NewLife goals? Is something important missing? If so, what changes and/or substitutions should I make?
- Do I have at least one strategy for each of my NewLife goals? Are my first-year strategies the best possible route to achieving my goals? Are there alternatives that might be better, quicker, cheaper, or more effective?
- Do I have at least one measurable objective for each of my NewLife goals? At the end of the first year, how will I measure my progress? What data will I use, and how will I collect it?
- Do my activities and tasks relate to my strategies? Is it clear that they will take me in the right direction in pursuit of my goals?

Based on your answers to the previous questions, make whatever changes you feel are appropriate to your NewLife Master Plan Summary. Then ask yourself this final question:

- Should I make any changes in my NewLife vision statement?

When you are satisfied with your NewLife Master Plan Summary, copy these two pages onto one 8½″ × 11″ page. Now your NewLife Master Plan Summary is on one page!

If you have followed the process described above, you should be happy with your NewLife Plan and the one-page summary. If you have made changes to your earlier material in creating your summary, go back now and make everything consistent. Doing the consistency review with the summary version makes it easier to spot problems and inconsistencies because everything is together in one place and you can see the *big* picture.

Seek Outside Review and Counsel

Up to this point, you have been creating your NewLife Master Plan Summary by yourself. The next step is to show it to the important people in your life who will be accompanying you on your journey and ask them for their reactions. Explain to them the process you have used, and ask them to review your summary for consistency, just like you did for yourself. You are *not* asking for validation of your vision or your goals, but rather for their opinions about how you plan to achieve them. Later on, you will follow the same process with your mentor, which is addressed in the following chapter.

How to Use Your NewLife Master Plan Summary

You now have your NewLife in perspective. Your one-page NewLife Plan Summary provides you with the focus you need to launch your NewLife. It describes who you are, where you want to go in your NewLife, and how you plan to get there. And all on one page!

So what do you do with it? We suggest that you post it in a prominent place where you are likely to see it every day, perhaps on the wall by your desk at home or on your refrigerator. You might even frame it or turn it into a screen saver for your computer. If you are still working, make a copy and carry it in your briefcase. Put it in a place where you will be exposed to it as often as possible in your daily routine so that you have a constant reminder. This will really help keep you focused.

Of course, your plans are never static. You will make changes to them as you change and as the world changes around you. Therefore, you will need a system for evaluating your progress and making course corrections along the way, the subject of Chapter 11.

Evaluating Your NewLife Progress and Making Course Corrections

John Trauth

Big shots are just little shots that kept shooting.

—CHRISTOPHER MORLEY,
EDITOR, AUTHOR

Now that you have your NewLife Master Plan, both the full plan and the one-page summary, let's take a moment to talk about how you will evaluate your progress and make course corrections.

Finding a Mentor

First, find someone to be your NewLife mentor. Ideally, this is someone who is a good friend but perhaps one you don't see on a regular basis. This will be a difficult step if, since becoming an adult, you have always made your own way in the world. Do it anyway, because the results will be well worth it. Think of it this way. Some highly placed professionals and CEOs hire life coaches to help them—and pay handsomely for their services. By following the NewLife Master Planning process, you are doing something similar and saving yourself big bucks at the same time! So power through your hesitations and pat yourself on the back.

Figure 11.1 is a job description for a NewLife mentor. You may want to share this job description with the person you are asking to be your mentor to insure that he or she understands the mentoring role and is willing to assume the responsibility.

Your NewLife mentor should not comment on your overall goals; those are your prerogative and should be taken as a given. Instead, ask your NewLife mentor to do the following:

- Review your NewLife plan, both the full and the summary versions, from an objective standpoint. Is there anything illogical about it? Is it too aggressive? Are you trying to do too much all at once? Will the strategies and objectives realistically lead to the accomplishment of the goals? Are the objectives measurable? Is there anything else that seems inconsistent?
- Meet with you six months from now and then again twelve months from now (and annually thereafter) to review your progress in accomplishing your goals and objectives. If you want more frequent feedback, ask to meet every six months rather than each year. Be sure to set the specific date after your first discussion, and set the date for the next meeting before ending the current one. Your mentor should keep a copy of your plan and review it before your next meeting. Together, you will discuss what went right, what went wrong, and what course corrections you should make.

Figure 11.1   **NewLife Mentor Job Description**

NewLife Mentor Job Description

Purpose:
To help keep me on track in my pursuit of my ideal retirement life, i.e., my NewLife

Activities:
- To review my NewLife vision and NewLife Master Plan, including my goals, strategies, objectives, and activities
- To accept and not criticize my vision and goals
- To meet with me as I begin this journey and discuss with me the following:
  - Is there anything illogical about my NewLife Master Plan?
  - Are my goals visionary and nonmeasurable?
  - Are my objectives measurable? Are they a logical extension of my goals?
  - Will my strategies logically lead to the achievement of my goals?
  - Will my activities help me achieve my objectives?
  - Am I too aggressive and unrealistic in what I'm trying to accomplish in the near future (five years, one year)?
  - Is there anything about my NewLife Master Plan that seems inconsistent?
- To discuss and review potential changes in my NewLife Master Plan
- To keep a copy of my revised NewLife Master Plan
- To agree to meet with me in six months and again in one year to review my progress and critique my updated NewLife Master Plan for the next period
- To keep all of our conversations on this matter strictly confidential

Remember that you are not looking for a critique of your goals, only of the methods you are using to attain them and the progress you are making toward realizing them. You can then, either with your mentor or by yourself, revise your goals if necessary and rewrite your strategies and objectives for the next period. When you are done, be sure to update your NewLife Master Plan Summary and put it back in its designated place. Send your mentor copies of everything in preparation for your next meeting.

Reviewing Your Progress

Go through each one of your goals with your mentor and determine the progress you have made. Are you on schedule? Have you achieved all or most of the objectives that you set for this date? Have your objectives and strategies moved you forward, or should you change them? What new strategies and objectives should you add to your plan?*

For example, if one of your goals was to learn to play tennis, and your one-year objective was to be playing local USTA matches competitively at the 3.0 level (intermediate), but after a year your USTA rating is 2.0 (just a little beyond beginner) and you still can't get a backhand over the net, you obviously haven't achieved your objective. There may be one or more reasons for this result:

- Something always came up the day of your tennis lesson, and you cancelled most of them.

---

*Be careful not to change too much too soon. Maybe your strategies are moving you toward your goals but you just had not given them enough time to work. Try to stick to your core strategies unless you find that they are truly flawed. If you give up on your strategies too soon, you may never reach your goals.

- You never made time to practice.
- You could never find someone to practice with.
- You have a difficult time understanding what your pro is trying to teach you.
- Your back hurts every time you play.
- You're a klutz, athletically, and would be better at basket weaving.

In this particular situation, you might ask yourself the following questions:

- Is playing at the 3.0 level still one of my priority objectives? If so, why have I cancelled most of my lessons, and/or why have I not found a practice partner and taken time to practice? What is this experience telling me about my priorities?
- If I do not feel that I am progressing with this particular tennis pro, should I still be taking lessons from him or her?
- Am I really cut out for this sport, or am I lacking something essential that I can't change and that will continue to keep me back (lack of eye-hand coordination, lack of mobility, bad eyesight, bad back, and so on).

There could, of course, be other reasons totally unrelated to the task at hand. Maybe Aunt Elsa died and, as her executor, you had to spend the last six months settling her estate. This might suggest you just delay your existing objectives. Or maybe you won the lottery, said forget tennis, and set off on a trip around the world. In the words of John Lennon, "Life is what happens while you're busy making other plans."

The point here is that the way you analyze the situation will suggest how to resolve it. If you are getting stuck, ask yourself why this is happening and then take action. But don't beat yourself up. If the situation is frustrating, if you are not making progress, if you are hurting yourself, if the solutions necessary to solve the problem seem difficult or impossible, or if you have higher priorities for your life, it may be time to end the frustration and set another goal. This is not failure. This is just realigning the path to success, because you are pursuing happiness and fulfillment, not frustration.

If you haven't achieved everything you set out to do, don't overreact. Most people do not even start on this journey. A large amount of your success will come from mere persistence. Big shots are just little shots who kept shooting.

At the same time, you should review your financial situation at least every six months, particularly if your investment strategy for your retirement involves a certain asset allocation, as we discussed in Chapter 8. It may be necessary to rebalance your portfolio, change the contribution mix (if you are still making contributions), or at least make some other minor adjustments. You should do this part with your financial advisor, not your mentor, unless he or she is both. Obviously, monitoring your financial situation is very important, and changes could suggest some modifications to your other goals and strategies. Everything in your plan is interrelated.

Maintaining Intensity

In your retirement years, you will have more opportunities to influence the intensity of your life. When you were working full-time, this was not totally under your control, at least not on the job. You may be looking forward to a more relaxed life now. And there is no reason why you can't have it.

But be careful. As Alan will discuss in the next chapter, there is a downside to too much relaxation. Personally, I like intensity. I like my life to be full of different challenges, and I like to make productive use of my time in pursuing my personal goals. I hope that your "dreams with deadlines" will give you a sense of intensity, or as much of it as you want. The trick is not to become frantic about pursuing your NewLife goals and objectives, at the same time as not becoming too lax because there is no longer anyone but your mentor reviewing your performance.

The answer is to find the level of intensity that you are comfortable with in your NewLife and build this into your plan. Finding this balance will probably take some time initially. You should get a feel for this as you review your progress in the first two or three sessions with your mentor. As you modify your goals and objectives, use this feedback to try to make your new NewLife Master Plan as realistic as possible, given the intensity with which you are comfortable. For example, you may be doing everything right in a certain area, but it just might take longer than you thought to get to a certain milestone, given the life that you want to lead. Even slow progress is progress, and if it is personally satisfying, you could consider continuing on a somewhat slower timetable.

Your semiannual and annual self-evaluations, with the help of your NewLife mentor, together with your financial reviews, will enable you to keep on course toward achieving your NewLife dreams. Keep your NewLife vision in your sights, and don't let little failures and frustrations get you down. By making these course corrections, your NewLife will only get better and better.

If you are optimistic, you will be able to see the potential good that might result from a situation, build it into your NewLife Master Plan, and work toward making it happen. If you don't look for these opportunities, you will probably miss them. And happiness results more from the pursuit than from the capture. We discuss this in more detail in Chapter 13.

Think of your NewLife as a journey, not a destination. Here is another way to think about it: an optimist and a pessimist will both ultimately arrive at the same dreary destination. (You can guess what that is.) But the optimist always wins, because he has enjoyed the journey.

Determining How You Want to Be Remembered

Alan Bernstein

*You make a living by what you get; you make
a life by what you give.*

—WINSTON CHURCHILL, STATESMAN,
BRITISH PRIME MINISTER

By now, we've discussed the choice to retire from multiple angles: the pragmatic issues, the plans you've made, the love and support you will require along the way, and the courage you'll need to take the leap. In this chapter, we will discuss this next stage of life from a more emotionally complex perspective and, in doing so, help you to proactively plan a legacy you can be proud of.

Changing Priorities, Reorganizing Goals

A successful transition to retirement can mean letting go of the individualistic uphill climb associated with functioning in a capitalistic society and embracing a more communal, lateral life. This may sound ironic, considering how we usually define the term *success*, but by leaving behind the trappings of personal ambition, a wider, more meaningful experience may await. Remember that you can now assume the role of the master, the dignified teacher. You can choose to be above the hustle and bustle of those coming up beneath you.

Simple enough, right? You're probably thinking that now you can sit by the pool and teach the grandkids how to swim. Actually, this transition is one of the more difficult aspects of retirement. Like most of us, up until this point you have viewed yourself romantically—as a person becoming ever more vital, an individual on the rise, a leader with unlimited potential. Could it really be that you've reached your peak? The giving up of the romantic self involves an overhaul of how you perceive yourself in relation to the world around you. Instead of struggling to climb to the top, you must now let go of that fight and reprioritize. This can be difficult, considering that you have spent your entire adult life working toward a future full of goals and ambitions. Now, in retirement, your goals and ambitions are more self-directed. Without the structure of your work environment and with no boss to answer to, why get out of bed in the morning? We hope that *Your Retirement, Your Way* will answer that question, and you will not want to disappoint your mentor or others by showing little or no progress toward your NewLife goals. But this may not be enough to motivate you. And therein lies the danger that must be overcome if your retirement years are to be rewarding.

All major life transitions have the potential of throwing us off course by changing the structure in which we have previously learned to function. The transition to retirement will be more difficult for those who spent most of their working life in a very structured environment, like a large company or organization, a university, or the government, and it will be less difficult for those who have had to bring their own structure to their work experience, like single practitioners, creative artists, professionals, or independent consultants. But it can be difficult for anyone.

Change Can Bring Surprising Feelings

I remember to this day the sense of fear and shame I felt when I decided to abandon my career as an English literature instructor at Rutgers University and pursue a new career as a psychotherapist. I found that my classroom personality was better suited to creating personal connections with my students and that the literary works I was exploring with them were vehicles to understand *them* as well as the texts. And I preferred understanding them! The shame I felt came from the sense that I was no longer a "success"—the youngest faculty member on Rutgers's staff. I was now entering a program—Master of Social Work—of dubious worth and little caché.

All I knew was that this program would license me to become a psychotherapist and entitle me to get the training and colleagueship I wanted. I tell you this, confessionally and conspiratorially, because I want you to understand that the drive that enabled me to make this switch was the force of my vision for my future. I knew what I wanted: a visceral sense of what I might feel and taste in the future that would enable me to bear the sense of loss and confusion that accompanied my vision. The conflicting emotions were intertwined—any one moment might bring visions of future glory or despair and loss.

I pursued the vision in spite of my fears of loss because I was convinced that I could create something better. But conviction does not carry us 24/7, and so I want to prepare you, particularly those of you who anguish over major decisions, to realize that vision and conviction do not mean protection against anxiety. The decision to give up that part of your identity that you have fostered through your work will at some moments be cheered as an opportunity and at others experienced as a loss. But if you reflect for a moment on your other life transitions, you will probably realize that they all created opportunities for you to renew yourself in different ways. Retirement offers that same opportunity now.

Developing Perspective

Changing your perspective from loss to opportunity can take some time. If you plan to continue working in the same field or for the same company on a part-time basis, it will be easier. But if you stop working entirely, it can be more of a shock, almost like losing a part of yourself. Most of us use our work environments to shape our personalities, and the reverse is also true.

Different Types of Retirees

What might lead you to be an "active" retiree, as opposed to an inactive one? An interesting perspective on this question is offered by Nancy K. Schlossberg in her book, *Retire Smart, Retire Happy: Finding Your True Path in Life*. Schlossberg, a counseling psychologist specializing in adult transitions, has broken down typical retiree behavior into five categories:

- **Continuers.**   Continuers are those who remain involved in the familiar, usually to a lesser capacity.

They include professors who now teach one class per year instead of three; and those who continue to serve on the board of directors at their companies, still making important decisions, but staying out of the "game." Continuers have a relatively comfortable transition, as their environment really hasn't changed. Along with this feeling of safety, however, comes a resistance to change, which could preclude great opportunity.

- **Adventurers.**   On the opposite spectrum, Adventurers see retirement as a chance to explore entirely new endeavors. They are the risk takers. Whether it's taking up mountain climbing or playing the piano, adventurers will be energized by their new passions. Along with the excitement, however, is the danger of failure if the new undertaking doesn't work out.
- **Searchers.**   Searchers meander along a path of interest and, reaching a dead end, try another path. By keeping an open mind, they explore many avenues looking for a fulfilling way to spend their time. Searchers keep their options open, which is a positive. The downside is the frustration that they may feel if time and again they become dissatisfied in their wanderings and never find their "true path."
- **Easy Gliders.**   Then there are those who have no set plan or goals, but take life one day at a time. Viewing each day as an open slate, the Easy Glider may get out of bed and visit with friends, go to water aerobics, or do whatever else suits his or her fancy. This freedom can be enticing, but watch out. Lack of structure and too much free time can lead to boredom.
- **Retreaters.**   Retreaters tend to pull back from their previous lives without reaching out to try new activities. Schlossberg maintains that a brief period of

"time out" after a lifetime of responsibility can be normal, such as that vacation we recommended that you take right after your retirement party. However, it is dangerous to withdraw too much and for too long. Disengaging from social interaction for a significant amount of time can lead to too much time in front of the television or, worse, chronic depression as life loses meaning and purpose.

Which category will you fall under when you retire? Actually, most of us will be a combination of one or more, but it can be helpful to realize that you might be inclined toward one or more of these "types" of retirees. According to Schlossberg, the only category to be really concerned about is the Retreater. The preretiree who is reading this book and preparing a NewLife Master Plan will more likely become the Continuer, the Adventurer, or the Searcher, or some combination of these types, seeking an active and growing experience in retirement. The Easy Glider probably sees no need for this book, and for the Retreater, it may already be too late.

However you define yourself during this transition, there will likely be some difficult moments. The tension you feel is the exchange of a "me-centered" life for a "we-centered" life. It is the act of choosing altruism over egotism. This is not simply a do-gooder mantra, a shallow idea to make you feel good about yourself. It is the way you can use your life experience for the betterment of others. It is literally a "win-win" situation, because you can benefit enormously by making this transition.

Much has been written about the 77 million "baby boomers" who are now approaching retirement and about how this

will create a major burden on society. A diametrically opposite view of the situation is offered by Marc Freedman. In his
book, *Prime Time: How Baby Boomers Will Revolutionize
Retirement and Transform America*, Freedman argues that
these 77 million people approaching their "post-midlife"
years can be a tremendous resource to change and
improve the world. Indeed, 50 percent of Americans
over age fifty are interested in "giving back" and plan to
incorporate volunteer service into later life. Not only will
society benefit in many ways from this great resource, but the
volunteers will stay connected, contribute to society, and get
to share and reaffirm the value of their own life experiences.
Freedman's book is full of examples of how meaningful and
fulfilling these experiences can be for retirees who take this
path.

Letting Go of Your Preretirement Existence

The letting go of your preretirement existence—your *self*,
even—will be challenging. It can feel like standing at the edge
of the unknown. Freedom can be found, however, if you
change the framework of how you have been thinking about
your life. Up until this point, you have been focused on moving ahead, on always getting more for yourself—more money,
respect, power, and even love.

In Chapter 5, we discussed the myriad ways to spend your
time once you choose to retire. Now, think about it in this
new context: which "me" activities can be most readily transformed into "we" activities? For example, one client of mine
who spent his working years as an accountant now gives free
financial advice to those in need. In this chart, list a few of
your "me" actions that could be translated to "we" actions.

Me	We

You may even be surprised to find that what you give back provides a stronger, richer vitality boost than your pre-retirement routines. Take the case of Evelyn and Michael, who successfully made the transition from "me" to "we."

After thirty years of working for the City of New York, Evelyn and Michael both had solid pensions that they could count on as they eased into retirement. Through their jobs, they had always been involved in the political and environmental workings of their Brooklyn neighborhood, Fort Greene. Now, they felt out of the loop and excluded without their exclusive access to information and people. Always people of action, curiosity, and drive, they wondered how they could continue to work for their community now that they were retired.

As they discovered, sometimes the solution is right under your nose. Evelyn and Michael live within a block of Fort Greene Park, the oldest park in Brooklyn. Over the decades, it had become run down and dangerous. It was no place to take the grandkids or stroll in the evening. "Why not join in the effort to restore the park to its former glory?" they thought. After all, they had many contacts around town who could be called upon to help. Today, the Fort Greene Park Conservancy is thriving, and full restoration of its lawns and historic monuments is set for completion in 2008. The estimated cost—$30–50 million—could not have been achieved without the help of Evelyn and Michael, who used the fund-raising skills they spent years acquiring to give back to their neighborhood.

What Is the Legacy You Want to Leave Behind?

Your accomplishments during the course of your career are nothing to be sniffed at. They may run the gamut from building your fortune to building a brand name to building your reputation. All worthy pursuits, but will they last? Are they the legacy you want to be known for years down the road? If the answer is "no," you are one step closer to making the mental switch from a "me" life to a "we" life.

By leaving behind the responsibilities you previously assumed, you now have the opportunity to take on an even more vital role with your family and community. It can be an exciting new beginning. This awareness—and responsibility, should you choose to accept it—will give you a solid dose of what I call "Viagra for the Soul." Laugh if you must, but the analogy applies. The invigoration you will feel when you accept that there is an alternative way of living can overcome your fear of feeling undervalued, of losing your position in society. Looking at the world in terms of "what can I give back" is a tremendously powerful place to be.

Making the World a Better Place

Imagine if all of the experts in the world, the masters who have excelled in their chosen arenas, applied themselves to making the world a better place for the next generation. Visualize the power of a mobilized force of men and women with something to say, something to teach, knowledge to impart. Why should our expertise lay fallow on the green of the local golf course? There's nothing wrong with an occasional game of golf, of course, but how much personal satisfaction can really be gained from it? Will the world be better for your putting skills? Will you? As Gandhi wisely put it, "The best way to find yourself is to lose yourself in the service of others."

But what does it mean to "lose yourself"? Doesn't that echo exactly what you fear the most when you contemplate retirement? Actually, the key is losing yourself *in* something, something bigger and better than you are. Remember the memories exercises you did in Chapter 3 when you recalled what you were doing when you were at your best. Think about what new memories like those you might be able to create now. I know one recent retiree who left it all behind to join Greenpeace. The last I heard, he was out chasing whale hunters in the North Atlantic, screaming his rage into the cold sea spray. That may sound extreme, but the point is clear: give back to something you care deeply about. That may be your local political arena or your place of worship or something else entirely. Whatever it is, if you energetically embrace the opportunity to give of yourself, you will be more likely to avoid the pitfalls that so many retirees succumb to, such as depression, family and marital problems, and a feeling of lack of purpose.

Using Your Talents

A word of warning. Once you find the cause or causes that you want to embrace, find the way that you can use your skills and talents to make the greatest contribution. This may take some time and perhaps some negotiation. Above all, don't let yourself be undervalued or underutilized, which will leave you frustrated and unfulfilled.

When John was asked to join the board of the local Big Brothers program, because of his work with foundations, he was assigned to the fund-raising committee. His first assignment was to go around to all the local stores and ask if they would agree to put a poster in their window for the upcoming fund-raiser, "Bowl for Kids' Sake." The development director was asking a management consultant who could make a big difference to the organization by cultivating his contacts and making a few phone calls to spend his weekends doing $10/hour work. John didn't say no. Instead, he hired a college student to do the work and asked him to return at the end of the day with a list of all of the stores he had visited and which ones had agreed to display the poster. When he got the list, John drove around for half an hour to make sure the posters were displayed. He then paid the student $70 for seven hours of work. When the development director asked John if he had completed his assignment, John gave him the list and told him what he had done. He also told the program director. The next year, John became the development director, and the year after, vice chair of the board, having raised considerable money for the organization using his skills and the skills of others in the appropriate manner.

Characteristics You Admire

Below, list a few people whom you admire (they can be personal or public figures) who worked to create positive change during the latter part of their lives.

Whose style of giving back would I feel most comfortable emulating? Why?

_____

_____

_____

_____

_____

_____

Now, circle the predominant characteristics that you would use in some type of community service.

Compassion	Leadership
Bravery	Honesty
Generosity	Patience
Kindness	Determination
Faith	Loyalty
Strength	Humor
Affection	

What types of pursuits do your attributes point you toward? List them here. (For example, if you circled Patience and Affection, it might make sense to volunteer to spend time with kids in need.)

Giving to Your Family

The legacy you choose to create can be defined by the work you do to effect positive change in your community and the world at large. In some cases, your legacy can be felt even more powerfully closer to home. By inspiring and giving time and love to our families, we can be certain that this giving of ourselves will be remembered and felt through those that we love the most.

A close friend was recently at a family reunion, and she and her cousins were discussing their great-grandparents. As with most oral histories, things got a bit blurry, but what she found interesting was how the legacies of these two people have carried on through the generations. Her great-grandmother had twelve children and lived well below the poverty line. Her kindness, self-sacrifice, and maternal strength are now the stuff of legend. She is still talked about with a sense of awe nearly a century later. On the other hand, her great-grandfather was a hard man, unloving and cruel. The legacy he left behind is not something any of them enjoys rehashing. His existence fades as his descendents choose to discuss brighter subjects at their gatherings.

A certain sense of immortality can be gained through our bloodlines. How do you want to be remembered in 2112? Imagine it's the wedding of your great-granddaughter, and a toast is being made to those who have passed on. In a brief paragraph below, describe how you would want your descendents to remember you after all of those years. What will be the legacy of your love?

Now, instead of dreading the transition to retirement or mindlessly approaching it as a long vacation, through adding community service to your Plan, you can look forward to major contributions you can make in the years ahead. By exchanging a self-centered existence for a life that revolves around a broader purpose, you are expanding both the vision and the purpose of your retirement. You are circumventing loss, overcoming fear of change, and taking on a position of power that has no limit.

Redefining Yourself

Dr. Sherwin Nuland, a clinical professor of surgery at Yale, takes a stand on this exact subject. His theory is that if people want to continue to feel vital and connected, they must "caress aging" and understand that, although there are negatives that come along with getting older, there are unforeseen pleasures as well. Here are his words from *Reflections on Life's Final Chapters*: "The getting and spending part of life is lessened, and the time for reflection is upon us—reflection and the small and large things we can do for others because we are less conflicted about relationships, rivalries, and the personal insecurities of our younger selves."

If you think about it this way, the struggle to redefine yourself may become a bit easier. You can even come out on the other side with a vitality that can be channeled into something great and lasting. And that can be how you will be remembered.

Christopher Chapman was a seventeenth-century philanthropist. Here are the words he had engraved on his tombstone:

> What I gave, I have.
> What I spent, I had.
> What I had left, I lost.

The French have a favorite saying, borrowed from Victor Hugo: "Qui donne aux pauvres, prête à Dieu." This means, "He who gives to the poor, lends to God."

Your contributions to society can and will contribute greatly to your legacy as well as to your own happiness and sense of fulfillment. We discuss this in more depth in the final chapter.

Living Happily Ever After

John Trauth

There are two things to aim for in life: first, to get what you want; and second, to enjoy it. Many achieve the first, but only the wisest achieve the second.

—LOGAN SMITH, AUTHOR

"And they lived happily ever after!" That's how many fairy tales end. And it is one of the reasons they are called fairy tales. It doesn't happen that way in real life. You have to continually work at it.

How do you become one of the wisest people who both get what they want and then also get to enjoy it? Thomas Jefferson and the founding fathers had it right when they wrote in the Declaration of Independence of our unalienable rights of "life, liberty and the *pursuit* of happiness." This final chapter will give you some suggestions about how to engage in that pursuit and "manage toward happiness and fulfillment" in your NewLife.

The Common Characteristics of Happiness

Let's start with some basics. Psychologists have found that people who are happy most of the time have these common characteristics:

- Self-approval
- Personal control of their lives
- Optimism
- Extroverted personality

Let's examine each of these in the context of your NewLife.

Self-Approval

Self-approval derives from high self-esteem. Self-esteem is an inner feeling of competence, relevance, and pride. It's about feeling good about who you are and having confidence in your ability to change your life. You cannot achieve lasting happiness and fulfillment without it. In your earlier years, while you were becoming who you now are, it was natural to compare yourself with your peers to see how you were doing and to use this comparison as a way to judge your progress. In addition, for most of your work years, you probably had a boss or a board of directors or investors or partners or others who were in a position to oversee your progress, evaluate your accomplishments, and give you feedback. By now, you know who you are, what you can and can't do, what you do and don't like, and you are no longer constantly comparing yourself with others. You may even have been the boss for a number of years, with others seeking your approval.

But after retiring, you will probably lose most of the structure, purpose and social network associated with your job, all of which reinforced your self-esteem. That is why it is critical to have a new purpose, a new structure with goals to accomplish, supportive friends and family, and a plan to do it. Your NewLife Master Plan gives you those things, and as you make progress toward your goals, your self-esteem and self-approval will be maintained and reinforced.

The philosopher John Stewart Mill was a determined proponent of the greatest happiness for the greatest number. "Ask yourself whether you are happy, and you cease to be so," he observed after recovering from a serious bout of depression. He finally came to believe that those who are truly happy "have their minds fixed on some object other than their own happiness; on the happiness of others, on the improvement of mankind, even on some art or pursuit, followed not as a means, but as itself an ideal end. Aiming thus at something else, they find happiness by the way."

Mother Teresa once said, "It is not a miracle that we do this work. The miracle is that we enjoy it."

Personal Control

When you retire, you assume more personal control of your life, so chances are that you now have that important characteristic. So unless someone else is still in control of your life, check that one off. But with control comes responsibility. Don't just let yourself drift. Use that control and your NewLife Master Plan to add back to your life the structure, community, and purpose that was previously provided by your work environment.

Optimism

Maybe you are not the most optimistic person. This doesn't mean that you are doomed to an unhappy life. But knowing that these traits are important for achieving happiness gives you important, useful information. If your early retirement experience is not positive, tell yourself to be optimistic—you can change your situation because you are now in control. Maybe you need a course correction, like we discussed in Chapter 11, but maybe instead you need an attitude correction. Optimism brings with it many benefits: lower stress, better health, greater self-confidence, better and stronger relationships, and more happiness and fulfillment.

Extroverted Personality

If you do not have a particularly extroverted personality, and after losing the social interaction with your work "community" you find yourself gradually evolving into the Retreater discussed in Chapter 12, actively seek ways to reconnect with others. Don't try to change your personality, but find your own ways to become more extroverted. For example, perhaps you can join a club, hobby group, or organization that does something you think is interesting or important. You can then go to functions and meet other people in the group with whom you already have a common interest. Maybe you can volunteer to be part of a group project. You could take a class in a subject that interests you at your local college or university extension and meet people there, or take an exercise class. Another way to connect would be to deepen your relationship with your family and friends. Ask them what projects they are involved with and, if something interests you, ask if you might join them and perhaps meet some of their friends.

If you are not inclined to join groups, you can be a mentor for someone else. Programs like Big Brothers Big Sisters offer wonderful opportunities to make a positive difference in a young person's life, and doing so will make a big difference in yours as well. It did for me.

You also know, from the earlier chapters, more about your personality and the situations in which you have done well in the past. Remember the flow exercises you did in Chapter 3? Why not try to find or create situations in retirement that may offer new "flow" possibilities? Think of it this way:

> *"Life is not measured by the number of breaths we take, but by the number of moments that take our breath away."*
>
> —ATTRIBUTION UNKNOWN

This does not mean that you should immediately take up skydiving or bungee jumping. Instead, it means that you should try to find projects and activities and create situations for yourself in which you can flourish, where you can get in the "flow" and use your talents and wisdom to make a contribution. Your own happiness will be the major by-product.

Adjusting to Both Adversity and Opportunity

You have made your plans for your NewLife. That's great. But the world is not always going to cooperate. Both good and bad things will happen. You can count on it. Life isn't fair, it's just life. How you cope with it makes the difference. That is why good business managers always try to see problems as opportunities. Try to do this in your own life.

In addition, unforeseen opportunities may arise at any time. They may not be part of your NewLife Master Plan. When they do, be opportunistic. Analyze and decide whether they are worthy of pursuing, and, before you say "yes," consider what else and who else you would be saying "no" to. In *Lifelaunch* terminology,* if you put these new opportunities into your "Take On" basket, what will you have to put into your "Let Go" basket? And how will you have to readjust your time allocations to accommodate the new opportunity? If pursuing the opportunity represents a significant change in your NewLife Master Plan, then before you make a final decision, discuss it with those people important in your life and get their agreement and support. Then revise your plan.

The reverse is also true. If you are not happy, particularly if you are stressed out and trying to do too much, remember the "Let Go" basket. Here is a personal example. One of the nonprofit boards on which I serve decided to take on a new, significant responsibility. Previously an oversight board, the organization assumed new obligations that required it to raise a significant amount of money over a period of years. This was an entirely new challenge for this board, and most members had never done this before. The beginning of the process was cumbersome, as the board made the wrong initial decisions, seeking to hire development staff to solve the problem. Instead, they should have been concentrating on developing the new vision for the organization and then doing a feasibility analysis to determine whether this vision would be saleable to potential supporters at the appropriate scale. If feasible, the next step would be to recruit the right campaign

---

*Frederic M. Hudson and Pamela McLean, *LifeLaunch: A Passionate Guide to the Rest of Your Life* (Santa Barbara, CA: The Hudson Institute Press, 1995.)

chairman, *then* to hire the development staff. It took a lot of work on my part to argue for this alternative approach.

Seeing the long struggle ahead and being involved in many other activities where things were going well and I was making a positive contribution, I decided to put this activity in my "Let Go" basket. While I still stay involved in a minimal fashion, I have been able to reduce my commitment and frustration considerably, freeing up my time and energy to concentrate on the positive contributions I can make elsewhere.

If you encounter such a situation, don't dwell on the negative experiences. Put them behind you and move on to bigger and better things. As Ingrid Bergman observed, "Happiness is good health and a bad memory."

Creating Your Own Reality

French and German existential philosophy is based on the assumption that life is not meant to be fair, it is meant to be life, and therefore it is how we deal with it that makes the difference. In the words of the Russian philosopher P. D. Ouspensky, "It is only when we realize that life is leading us nowhere that it begins to have meaning."

While you may reject this perspective, there is a lesson here. Whether you are an existentialist, a highly religious person, or somewhere in between, it is critically important to bring structure and purpose to your NewLife, which is what the exercises in the previous chapters are designed to do. You are essentially creating your own reality. If you don't like that reality, change it! Instead, fill your NewLife with things you enjoy. And keep the structures in place that have provided support for you in the past, such as your church or synagogue, your athletic or social club, your volunteer work, and your membership in other organizations. If you change your residence in retirement, seek to rebuild these structures in your new location while maintaining your previous friendships, even if it is by snail mail, e-mail, or long-distance phone calls.

My favorite poem on creating your own reality is "Renascence" by the American lyrical poet Edna St. Vincent Millay. Here is how she expresses the concept:

> *The world stands out on either side*
> *No wider than the heart is wide;*
> *Above the world is stretched the sky—*
> *No higher than the soul is high.*

Enjoying Your NewLife Guilt Free

You may feel some guilt when you first begin your NewLife. This is normal, and a common feeling early in retirement. You are not working as hard or at all, and you are not contributing to society in the same way as you did before. You may even be doing some things that do not seem "productive" in terms of society's definition of productivity.

Voltaire once said, "The superfluous is absolutely necessary." You never can tell where some of these superfluous activities may eventually lead. Was it superfluous for me to go on a camping trip with Alan after just getting back from a yearlong vacation in France? It may have seemed so at the time, but the camping trip and my willingness to take the Birkman® personality profile helped me to better understand myself and subsequently reinvent myself in retirement—and eventually led to the writing of this book.

Obviously, you don't want all of your activities to be superfluous or you risk evolving into irrelevancy. That is why we have continually counseled you to find ways to remain involved and to continue to make a contribution. But enjoy your "nonproductive" activities, too. Who knows where they will lead? As you begin this journey, think of yourself as the "outward bound" explorer, as defined in the Outward Bound brochure:

> Outward Bound signifies that moment when a ship leaves its mooring and commits itself to the open sea with all its unknowns, hazards and adventures. It is a recurring demonstration of human nobility and of our desire to seek and determine our own destiny, no matter what the challenge.

Finally, seek to understand what you can control and what you cannot, and put your effort into the former, not the latter. Remember Reinhold Niebuhr's famous saying: "God grant me the serenity to accept the things I cannot change; the courage to change the things I can; and the wisdom to know the difference."

Or, as an anonymous writer put it: "If you want to be happy, put your effort into controlling the sail, not the wind."

Simplifying Your Life

In this day and age, most of us live a very complicated existence. Your work life probably contributed to this. Moving into retirement, many of these complications may no longer be necessary. For example, do you really need multiple computers or six different ways for people to contact you? Maybe you need a little peace and quiet instead, and some time for genuine thought and reflection.

Try this: Select a week and, starting on Monday, resolve to do one thing each day to simplify your life. For example, find ways to eliminate unnecessary activities and stress. Consolidate bills or outsource your bill-paying entirely. Do you really need that extra cell phone? Are there other assets that demand your attention but that you actually no longer need? Maybe you have been involved with a board, a religious organization, or some other volunteer effort for too many years and feel burned out. You will be amazed at how liberated you will feel as you rid yourself of these unnecessary obligations. By simplifying, you are also adding time to your life to pursue your goals and achieve your NewLife vision. Set aside a "simplification week" once or twice a year.

Living in the Present

Your Retirement, Your Way has obviously been a book about planning your future. Planning ahead with defined goals, objectives, and time frames helps you bring focus, structure, and purpose to your retirement life. In addition, the anticipation of good things to come adds significantly to their enjoyment. In *Stumbling on Happiness*, Daniel Gilbert postulates that more than 50 percent of enjoyment comes from anticipation. Consequently, I never leave France without setting a date for a return trip.

But you can't live in the future any more than you can live in the past. As we have suggested, you can learn from the past and use those lessons to plan for your future. But you have to live in the present and live every day the best you possibly can.

An excellent book on his subject is *The Power of Now,* by Eckhart Tolle. He argues that living in the moment relaxes us, lowers our stress levels, and is crucial for living happily.

The Indian dramatist, Kalidasa, in his poem "Salutation to the Dawn," wrote, "For yesterday is but a dream / and tomorrow is just a vision, / And today well lived makes every yesterday a dream of happiness / And every tomorrow a vision of hope. / Look well, therefore to this day!"

And while you are living in the present, make a special effort to appreciate your life and what you already have. The more you appreciate what you have, the less you will want or need.

Living Up to Your Potential

Even though you are working less or not at all, always try to live up to your personal potential in whatever you do. But don't interpret this advice as constant pressure to always be an overachiever. Rather, see it more in a long-term context of pursuing the happy life that you wrote about in your retirement vision. Abraham Lincoln once said, "I am not bound to win, I am bound to be true. I am not bound to succeed, but I am bound to live up to the light that I have."

And always remember that you are not alone in your journey. Discuss your happiness with your spouse/significant other, family, friends, and mentor. Tell them how you feel, how it's going, and what you like and don't like about your NewLife. Get their opinions. Seek their advice. If your realignments and course corrections will change their lives as well, get their buy-in, too, because if they are not happy, chances are that you will not be, either. If it still is not working, seek professional help from a professional life coach or a psychotherapist. Attend a "Your Retirement, Your Way" workshop or retreat (see our website, yourretirementyourway.com for schedules and details) or participate in other life-transition seminars. The interaction with others in similar circumstances could provide you with the insights you need. Invest both the time and money to learn how to remove the obstacles to your happiness and replace them with happiness opportunities. The return on this investment will be enormous. In the end, this is really what it is all about.

Managing Toward Happiness and Fulfillment

To summarize, here are the ways to manage toward happiness and fulfillment in your NewLife:

- Create situations in which you can flourish and make a contribution.
- Try to see problems as potential opportunities.
- Get buy-in for major NewLife changes from those closest to you.
- Focus on making other people happy.
- Get rid of things that are making you unhappy.
- Don't dwell on negative experiences.
- Be optimistic that you can change your life for the better.
- Don't beat yourself up if things take longer than you think.
- Seize new opportunities when they arise.
- Stay involved and connected to your family and community.
- Enjoy your nonproductive time and activities without feeling guilty.

- Take steps to simplify your life.
- Live in the present.
- Appreciate what you already have.
- Always strive to live up to your potential.

The Journey Ahead

If you have not just read the chapters but have also done the exercises carefully and thoughtfully, you now have your NewLife Master Plan and are well prepared to begin your retirement journey. You know yourself better, what your needs are and what motivates you, and you know how to create situations in which you will flourish. In addition, you have envisioned your ideal retirement and created your plans for your NewLife. You have sufficient support from your family, friends, community, and mentor. You know how to arrange your finances to support your NewLife. You also know how to make course corrections along the way and manage your life to achieve happiness. You have even thought about the legacy you want to leave behind. Compared to the vast majority of others approaching retirement, you are *much* better prepared, both psychologically and strategically, to create a unique NewLife for yourself in which you will be able to expand your horizons and to continue to learn and grow and thrive. Congratulations!

Now, go do it! Create and live the life of your dreams! Alan and I wish you good luck and Godspeed on your journey. We leave you with these simple words from Jonathan Swift:

May you live all the days of your life.

Resources

Books

The authors would like to acknowledge the contributions of the many other authors quoted in this book whose ideas have increased the power of many readers to plan for, inform, and enrich their life transitions, including retirement.

Astre, Patrick P. *This Is Not Your Parents' Retirement: An Inspirational Guide to Investment for a Revolutionary Generation.* (Irvine, CA: Entrepreneur Press, 2005.) This book is a guide for people who want to build and preserve wealth toward retirement. Topics covered include mutual funds, stocks, bonds, insurance products, tax strategies, debt management, setting up future streams of income, and real estate investing.

Bachrach, Bill. *Values-Based Financial Planning: The Art of Creating an Inspiring Financial Strategy.* (San Diego: Aim High Publishing, 2000.) This book about personal finances focuses on awareness of your values and making investment choices consistent with this knowledge. Readers create their own financial road map to implement their values-based financial strategy.

Birkman, Roger. *True Colors: Get to Know Yourself and Others Better with the Highly Acclaimed Birkman Method®.* (Thomas

Nelson, Inc., 1995.) This book is an in-depth introduction to the Birkman Method® by its founder and creator. Roger covers personal relationships, spiritual values, and life transitions. If your aim is to enter this period of your life with grace and equanimity, this book will engage you.

Bolles, Richard N. *What Color Is Your Parachute? A Practical Manual for Job-Hunters and Career-Changers.* (Berkeley, CA: Ten Speed Press, 2006.) If you think of your retirement as a new career (which in many ways it is), this is the book to help clarify your skills, interests, needs, and style. Beyond the career horizons, Dick understands the pace of change and engages the reader to maintain a process of self-respect through major transitions.

Crowley, Chris, and Henry S. Lodge. *Younger Next Year: A Guide to Living Like 50 Until You're 80 and Beyond.* (New York: Workman Publishing Company, 2004.) A doctor and a retired litigator team up to present a personal story and a passionate argument that if you train for the next third of your life, you can live with vitality and grace well into your later years. Biological and evolutionary research is combined with pragmatic advice about maintaining active physical and intellectual lifestyles to stay young in body and mind.

Csikszentmihalyi, Mihaly. *Flow: The Psychology of Optimal Experience.* (New York: Harper Perennial, 1990.) A rare ability to manage a transcendent idea and make it applicable to everyday life is the source of the joy waiting within this book. Highly recommended as a beginning source to understanding the power of epiphanies. Dr. Csikszentmihalyi trains the reader to both recognize and appreciate the power of the moment.

Edmunds, Gillette, and Jim Keene. *Retire on the House: Using Real Estate to Secure Your Retirement.* (Hoboken, NJ: John Wiley & Sons, 2005.) This book describes how to use your home equity to finance your retirement. Strategies include selling your home and moving to a less expensive residence, remodeling your home into units for rental income, home equity conversion loans, and reverse mortgages.

Freedman, Marc. *Prime Time: How Baby Boomers Will Revolutionize Retirement and Transform America.* (HarperCollins Canada/Public Affairs, 2000.) Countering the negative implications associated with the large number of retiring baby boomers and what a drain this will be on society, Freedman takes the opposite, optimistic view that baby boomers can be an enormous resource for improving society through volunteer work with nonprofit organizations. The book argues that volunteer work can bring greater fulfillment and purpose to the "postmidlife" years.

Gilbert, Daniel. *Stumbling on Happiness.* (New York: Random House, 2006.) A Harvard psychologist presents the latest research on happiness and reveals what scientists have discovered about the uniquely human ability to imagine the future and our capacity to predict how much we will like it when we get there.

Goleman, Daniel. *Emotional Intelligence: 10th Anniversary Edition.* (New York: Random House/Bantam, 2005.) This seminal book helped create a national dialogue about the nature of intelligence: what it is, how it is best applied, and its connection to creativity and social relationships. If any of those questions appeal to you, so will this book.

Horan, Jim. *The One Page Business Plan: Start with a Vision, Build a Company.* (Berkeley, CA: One Page Business Plan Company, 2004.) Presented as a professional planning tool for entrepreneurs, this book helps simplify the complex process of creating a business plan. Clearly written, with helpful examples, friendly visual graphics and humor, Jim helps small businesses focus on what is important to building a successful business. This book will also be useful for preretirees looking to transform a hobby into a money-making venture in retirement. Now comes with CD-ROM.

Hudson, Frederic M., and Pamela McLean. *LifeLaunch: A Passionate Guide to the Rest of Your Life.* (Santa Barbara, CA: The Hudson Institute Press, 1995.) The book examines life transitions and renewal cycles and provides tools for proactively approaching change during the adult years. Effective strategies for life transitions are presented to help lead to personal growth and fulfillment.

Lindquist, Peter. *Solving the Retirement Puzzle: How to Get the Most out of the Rest of Your Life.* (Lafayette, CO: Moonlight Publishing, 2005.) This book provides forty anecdotal examples of retirees who overcame the challenges they faced in retirement. Key topics include the importance of preparing financially; maintaining physical, mental, and spiritual health; revitalizing relationships; and maintaining self-esteem.

Morgenstern, Julie. *Time Management from the Inside Out: The Foolproof System for Taking Control of Your Schedule and Your Life.* (New York: Owl Books, 2004.) Offering a three-step program—Analyze, Strategize, Attack—this book provides time management techniques to help reclaim your life from your busy schedule. It helps you define your goals in life and explains how to reorganize your time to help achieve them. It also includes helpful time-mapping tools to help you determine where you invest too much and too little time.

Pollan, Stephen M., and Mark Levine. *Second Acts: Creating the Life You Really Want, Building the Career You Truly Deserve.* (New York: HarperCollins, 2003.) Written for everyone from the twenty-five-year-old career-changer to the sixty-five-year-old almost-retiree, this book describes how to successfully change the course of your life and create a more rewarding, enjoyable future. The authors argue that most of the barriers to a rich and rewarding life are self-imposed and surmountable.

Schlossberg, Nancy K. *Retire Smart, Retire Happy: Finding Your True Path in Life.* (Washington D.C.: American Psychological Association, 2003.) The author interviewed one hundred men and women and categorized them by the types of paths they followed. Five categories of retirees emerged from the research: Continuers, Adventurers, Searchers, Easy Gliders, and Retreaters. Most people follow a combination of paths and may change courses at different points in their retirement years.

Shapiro, David. *Retirement Countdown: Take Action Now to Get the Life You Want* (Indianapolis, IN: Pearson/FT Prentice Hall,

2004.) A financial-planning book focused on retirement issues and strategies, including saving for retirement; establishing an income you can't outlive; understanding and managing investment risks; and investing in equity and fixed income investments, mutual funds, insurance, and annuities.

Stein, Ben, and Phil DeMuth. *Yes, You Can Still Retire Comfortably! The Baby Boom Retirement Crisis and How to Beat It.* (Carlsbad, CA: New Directions Press, 2005.) This book focuses on retirement financial planning, including investing for retirement, how much to save and how much to spend, strategies for drawing down retirement savings, and what to do if everything you have is not enough. Fall-back strategies include immediate annuities, moving to another location, and reverse mortgages.

Tolle, Eckhart. *The Power of Now: A Guide to Spiritual Enlightenment.* (Novato, CA: New World Library, 2004.) Not aligned with any particular religion or tradition, this book emphasizes the importance of living life in the present; freeing oneself from dominance of the analytical mind; and achieving a calm sense of presence, "being," and spirituality.

Updegrave, Walter. *We're Not in Kansas Anymore: Strategies for Retiring Rich in a Totally Changed World.* (New York: Random House/Crown Business, 2004.) This book describes the realities associated with financial retirement planning in today's world. Employers are cutting back company pension plans and replacing them with individually directed 401(k) plans; the long-term future of Social Security is in doubt; and individuals need to take more responsibility for planning their own financial future. This book provides detailed and helpful advice about saving and investing to secure your future.

Watzlawick, Paul, John Weakland, and Richard Fisch. *Change: Principles of Problem Formation and Problem Resolution.* (New York: W. W. Norton & Company, Inc., 1974.) This book provides a valuable demonstration of how to apply the principles of mathematics and logic to any problem, whether theoretical or functional. It is concerned with how problems arise and how they are perpetuated in some instances and resolved in others.

It examines how, paradoxically, common sense and "logical" behavior often fail and provides guidance in converting "stuck issues" into a series of resolvable steps.

Yolles, Ronald M., and Murray Yolles. *Getting Started in Retirement Planning.* (Hoboken, NJ: John Wiley & Sons, 2000.) A broad financial-planning guide covering a number of topics, including saving for retirement, life stage financial strategies, investing while retired, protecting your portfolio, health care, and estate planning.

Zelinski, Ernie J. *How To Retire Happy, Wild, and Free: Retirement Wisdom That You Won't Get from Your Financial Advisor.* (Berkeley, CA: Ten Speed Press, 2004.) This book offers advice about how to enjoy life to the fullest in retirement, including finding interesting leisure activities and creative pursuits; traveling; achieving physical and mental well-being; and the importance of a balanced life with strong social support.

Other Resources

Birkman Method® (birkman.com)   To utilize the full Birkman Method®, contact Birkman International (800-215-2760). They will put you in contact with a Birkman® consultant in your area. The Birkman Method® consists of many different applications, and you may select the specific areas that are most significant to you.

Hudson Institute (hudsoninstitute.com)   Located in Santa Barbara, California, this learning center is dedicated to developing capacities for change. The concept of the "Renewal Cycle" is examined and explained. Workshops and training programs are offered that are specifically focused on the transition to retirement.

North Carolina Center for Creative Retirement (unca.edu/ ncccr) Located at the University of North Carolina at Asheville, the center was early to recognize the coming seismic shift in the aging U.S. population and has been in the forefront of research and course offerings on retirement. As baby boomers age and the median U.S. age increases, the center continues to study the effect on the U.S. economy, the job market, nontraditional work patterns, and other emerging trends.

Outward Bound (outwardbound.org)   This organization originated from the concept that we are more capable of extraordinary motivation and behavior than most of us realize. To go on an Outward Bound expedition is to give yourself license to see the world through new eyes, renewing your optimism about the joy of change, which can help facilitate the transition to retirement.

Road Scholar (roadscholar.com)   Educational travel is gaining popularity as a vacation with a difference, and among the best is Road Scholar, an offshoot of Elderhostel. Designed for retired and soon-to-retire professionals, Road Scholar focuses on in-depth learning in a new culture, with insights provided by experts. Adventure trips run by Steve Van Beek are specifically recommended. Steve, a forty-year resident of Asia, author, and river explorer, and his wife, Piyawee Ruenjinda, take visitors down lesser-known rivers of Southeast Asia on journeys of three to seventeen days. These are no-strain, no-hurry adventures to absorb local cultures and settings. They include hikes, overnights in village homes, and a chance to experience and share rural life. For a schedule of upcoming trips as well as photos from past trips, visit stevevanbeek.com.

Our Seminars and Websites

Guide to Your Career (guidetoyourcareer.com)   This website was initially designed for college students beginning their career adventure. However, it has been widely adopted by career changers of all ages, and if you accept the paradigm of retirement as a new career/transition, this will likely be a resource for you as well.

Your Retirement, Your Way (yourretirementyourway.com)   Our official website provides information on our seminars, references to other retirement resources, and publication and content updates on retirement planning.

Index

About the Authors

Alan Bernstein is a psychotherapist practicing in New York City. He received his B.A. from the University of Michigan, spent a peripatetic year in Europe, completed his course work for his Ph.D. in English Literature at Rutgers University, and was appointed its youngest faculty member. Alan soon realized he was in the wrong profession and began the process of "conscious decision making" exemplified in this book. He went back to school—supported by a National Institute of Mental Health Fellowship—and received his M.S.W. from Yeshiva University, beginning a career consulting to private agencies and New York's Metropolitan Hospital while maintaining faculty appointments at New York Medical College (Psychiatric Residency Training) and the New York University Graduate School (Post-Masters and Doctoral Programs in Psychotherapy). Thus began his professional exploration of life transitions, accessing creative resources to energize bold moves. His book, *Princeton Review's Guide to Your Career*, is now in its sixth edition. While continuing his private psychotherapy practice, Alan is also an organizational development consultant for financial service companies, and he serves on three nonprofit advisory boards that touch the lives of disadvantaged New Yorkers: Creative Alternatives of New York, Publicolor, and Camp Interactive. He believes that the process of transition, though daunting, can be cultivated and become an adventure in itself.

John Trauth is a management consultant in San Francisco. He graduated from Colgate University and received his M.B.A. from the Amos Tuck School at Dartmouth College. After graduate school, he and a buddy toured Europe for six months on motorcycles, camping out on the French Riviera and the Greek islands. He moved to San Francisco in 1968 to work as a management consultant and found he was best suited to the financial services industry, particularly community finance. As his career evolved, he eventually specialized in creating innovative financing programs for affordable housing and small business development. After retiring in 1995, he and his wife Astrid moved to France for a year where he enrolled at the Sorbonne to study French language, culture, and civilization. On returning to San Francisco, he reinvented himself as a part-time management consultant specializing in strategic planning and affordable housing. His clients include banks, nonprofits, and cities. In his volunteer work, he is president of the Olympic Club Foundation, which raises money and provides funding for athletic programs serving disadvantaged youth throughout the Bay Area. He also serves on three other nonprofit boards as well as on the Advisory Council of the Graduate School of Business Management at the University of San Francisco. He and his wife live in Sausalito and spend a month a year in Paris, consistent with their NewLife Master Plan.